AS LONG AS LIFE

The Memoirs of a Frontier Woman Doctor

**Mary Canaga Rowland, M.D.
Edited and with
a Foreword by
F. A. Loomis**

FAWCETT CREST • NEW YORK

A Fawcett Crest Book
Published by Ballantine Books
Copyright © 1994, 1995 by Carolyn Madsen Williams and F. A. Loomis

http://www.randomhouse.com

Originally published by Storm Peak Press in 1994.

Library of Congress Catalog Card Number: 95-96232

ISBN 0-449-22511-9

Manufactured in the United States of America

First Ballantine Books Edition: May 1996

10 9 8 7 6 5 4 3 2 1

Contents

Foreword

"I watched through the rafters of our sod house attic an autopsy performed on the family table. I was eight years old in Red Willow. No one saw me watching. Neighbors requested the autopsy on the body of a man who died under unusual circumstances. I don't remember who did the dissection, or what was found as a result."

—MARY CANAGA ROWLAND, M.D.

This story fragment is among those of my great-great-aunt that are still shared orally in the family. Other stories of hers are recorded in the following memoirs she wrote from 1930 to 1955. Born in Nebraska on June 29, 1873, Mary grew up on the prairie and went on in Kansas, Missouri, and Nebraska to obtain two medical degrees because of her fascination with human anatomy.

She married a Kansas doctor who was also a lawyer and a teacher, and they practiced together until tragedy ended their marriage in 1902. Mary's medical practice spanned developments from after the Civil War to the early twentieth century and her writ-

ings mingle personal experience with larger events of
the time.

From a girl marveled by violent prairie thunder-
storms, Mary lived to see newsreels about atomic
weapons. Once afraid of Indian raids on her family's
Nebraska homestead, she became an Indian school
doctor involved in the lives of children of many
tribes.

The reader will find here a physician of strong will
who practiced freely before the passage of women's
suffrage, tried to join the army as a doctor during the
Mexican-American crisis, and selected medical offices if they could also serve as homes for her daughter. She married a man who was intellectually her
equal and gave her a deed to a house instead of a
wedding ring.

Mary's memoirs include case studies of childbirth,
disease, mental illness, suicide, incest, and adoption.
She points out that narcotics laws came into exis-
tence too late to curb the free use of drugs by un-
stable physicians, one of whom she knew to be a
morphine addict. She relates her effort and failure to
reform a young con artist upon whom she took pity.
She also talks about a few friends, including a kind,
world-traveling bum; a Siwash Indian woman, probably one of the last of her tribe; and a woman who
came to Lebanon, Oregon, as a man.

Her stories include descriptions of attitudes toward
doctors, the miracle workers on the plains who were
also scapegoats if anything went wrong. The typical
country doctor in the early twentieth century battled
public ignorance of medicine, caprices and frauds of
quacks, and superstitions of religious zealots.

Men were largely unreceptive to women doctors during Mary's years of medical practice. She executed her duties despite resistance from arrogant husbands of female patients who distrusted women doctors and dictated procedure during childbirth or illness. It was probably harder for her to tolerate the self-important male doctors who did not disguise their contempt for a woman practitioner. No doubt her diagnostic shrewdness and genuine care for patients intimidated many male doctors. This is not to overlook the fact that she enjoyed good relationships with other male surgeons and physicians.

Mary quoted Gertrude Stein and William Shakespeare and was unashamed of her delight in reading James Fenimore Cooper's fantastic Leatherstocking Tales. Her stories include typical western images of buffalo, wagon trains, and gunfights, as well as her plainswoman's impressions of New York City and Union Square during one of that city's greatest immigration periods.

Mary had a broad set of interests. She studied graphic arts and took extension courses in batik from the University of Oregon. At one point she did block printing using old naval battleship linoleum. She won premium ribbons at the Oregon State Fair for her artwork and managed to sell some of these pieces. One brought her what she regarded as a high price while on display at a museum in Chicago.

She began to care full-time for her granddaughter Carolyn Madsen in 1939, and after raising Carolyn retired to a more sedentary lifestyle. Mary died in Salem, Oregon, on August 1, 1966, at ninety-three years of age.

Some readers may be curious about what Mary— like many overly discreet men and women of her age—did not tell us in her memoirs. As these repressed elements required considerable research, the book is presented in co-author fashion, with editorial commentary in italics.

Other readers may focus on her subtleties of expression that reveal greater or lesser degrees of social enlightenment. Every effort was made to preserve the author's original voice. In this respect, some terms that may indicate bias were retained throughout the editing process.

To make the text consistent chronologically, it was necessary to reorganize and divide it into chapters. Some fragments of the material were deleted because of their irrelevance to the primary story line, incompleteness, or redundancy. Most of the archaic spelling was updated and confusing syntax untangled. The disjointed transitions in Mary's episodic storytelling style were softened. Although it has been impossible to liberate readers entirely from this style of presentation, it becomes less noticeable after the first several chapters.

As Mary's great-great-nephew, I visited her as a boy and remember her powerful visage. It has been, however, mostly through her writings and her daughter Nellie, granddaughter Carolyn, and my grandfather—mentioned in the text as Floyd—that I know her. With this publication others will have the opportunity to read Mary's story, a portion of one family's saga traceable to the Revolutionary War.

—F. A. LOOMIS

Red Willow

I was born in 1873 in Red Willow during the incubating period of the modern world. Nebraska was a pioneer state with western counties in "The Great American Desert," a vast grassy plain covered with grama and buffalo grass. Here and there were muddy streams.

> *The Great American Desert was depicted on many maps used in American schoolbooks until about 1860. Mary's contemporary Willa Cather was also born in 1873, in Virginia, and moved to Red Cloud, Nebraska, nine years later.*

The grasses were rich in food value and nourished buffalo, and later cattle. It was nearly a treeless country, with trees only along the streams: box elder, elm, ash, hackberry, willow, cottonwood, and an occasional cedar. In good seasons there were wild plums, chokecherries, elderberries, and grapes; also sumac and the wild rose, the sensitive plant whose leaves curled when you touched them.

The most beautiful time of the year was May when the wind quieted down and the green grasses peeped through the old tawny grasses of the previous year. In memory I hear a meadowlark with its joyous song, and the creak of harness as the horses pull the plow along. I see the rich dark loam as it curls up from the plow. I hear my father's voice as he follows, row on row.

It is all plains country from the Gulf of Mexico to Hudson Bay and the wind has a clean sweep blowing nearly all the time. Sometimes the wind blew up violent storms, blowing and blowing for days until a faint outline appeared on the horizon. As a day wore on, this shadow grew and advanced rapidly until great jagged tongues of lightning flickered up and down.

Suddenly the wind died and all the land seemed as still as death, then with a mighty roar that great black cloud filled the whole world with wind, rain, thunder, and lightning so that every living thing sought shelter from its fury. There was great destruction from the violence of the wind, rain, and hail. But in thirty minutes the storm always passed. Then a drop of rain came, and soon the stars peeped out.

In southwestern Nebraska, we were in danger of raids by the Sioux Indians who were unfriendly to the white settlers. The U.S. government had a company of soldiers at Fort Kearney on the Platte River to discourage the Indians. Nevertheless, they made a few raids. They shot one of our distant neighbors, Mr. Stenner, who lived with his family on Beaver Creek. Three Indians rode up to his door and asked for some tobacco and when he came out they shot him. His wife and children found refuge in the creek, standing in water up to their necks all day under some willows. At night they made their way to a neighbor's house. I saw Mrs. Stenner many times in later years.

*In the late 1870s the number of incidents in Nebraska
between settlers and plains Indians was rapidly de-
creasing. In 1871, however, Mary's mother Ellen was
visited by Indians just after her first daughter, Mary's
sister May, was born. Ellen's story is cited in Ida C.
Miles'* Echoes of the Plains, *privately printed in
1950:* "I was standing in the door just glancing
around and wondering when Mr. Canaga would get
home when I looked up the road and saw seventeen
Indians coming toward the house. They were riding
ponies and had feathers on their heads and were
painted in bright colors. . . . I was so frightened my
heart almost quit beating. I didn't know what to do.
There I was alone with my baby. I also knew that the
soldiers had been moved from Republican City and
there was no protection in the neighborhood. There I
was without a gun in the house. I looked at the baby
in the cradle and wondered what I could do to protect it. I thought of the stories I had heard about how
cruel Indians had been to children.

"I thought of an old pair of sheep shears that we
had, and they were very sharp. I ran and got them
and hid them under the cradle. I decided if we had to
die, I would not give up without getting one of them,
too.

"I sat down by the cradle . . . waiting to die. My
heart seemed to quit beating as the baby slept on.
They came to the door and said something rough. I
could not understand them. Then they walked into the
house. . . . I thought by the way they acted they were
hungry and wanted something to eat. They looked in
the box cupboard and in the flour barrel, and all
around the room. . . . One of them . . . motioned to his

mouth and said, 'Melons.' I told them where the melon patch was so they would go away. They all left the room and went out to the melon patch. How glad I was, for I thought now I am rid of them.

"I stayed by the cradle and watched. After awhile I saw them coming back and thought that they were coming back to kill me. . . . One of the Indians . . . gave a whoop and waved his arm. . . . I grabbed the sheep shears again . . . [but] he ran past the door and out into the melon patch and then returned . . . swinging a large tomahawk [that he had forgotten] and said as he passed the door, 'Good paleface squaw.' I cannot express how I felt."

For a number of years our nearest store was at Fort Kearney, nearly two hundred miles away, but a trading point was soon established at Plum Creek, now Lexington. As the community grew, the little town of Indianola was raised along Coon Creek, some six miles from our homestead. It was the county seat for many years.

Many of the settlers were Civil War veterans as was my father, my mother's brother William Crockford, and Russell Loomis. Politically, the neighborhood was predominantly Republican, but we had one neighbor from Texas and his wife from Kentucky, the Longneckers. John Longnecker was at the time a Democrat. At first my folks were very suspicious of the Longneckers. The Civil War had been too recent. It didn't seem to my people that anyone good could come out of the South. As time passed, however, we became intimate friends. I suppose that common hardships and common problems always knit people together.

Many of the veterans in Red Willow County were getting pensions, and my mother had long tried to persuade my father to apply for one. He didn't want to for he liked to feel he didn't need it, but we were so short of money that he finally did and the U.S. government allowed him the munificent sum of eight dollars a month. It was not much but it was something. There were many places for every cent.

As there was little money, the neighbors exchanged work with one another. And if someone was ill, a neighbor was always there to help care for the sick or do the required chores.

Mother took care of women in confinement. She delivered the baby, took care of mother and baby, and in addition did the housework and cooked for the rest of the family for up to two weeks, all for five dollars a week. Usually she stayed only one week.

Mother had two books on midwifery that she kept hidden from the family. I used to look at them when no one was around and think, "What queer pictures!"

At one point, my folks mortgaged our homestead for five hundred dollars to buy cattle. I asked my father how he was going to pay it off and he said, "Well, I guess you can teach school by that time and pay it off." I counted the years until the mortgage was due and realized I would only be thirteen. I just knew I wouldn't know enough by then to teach school. Of course, my father was joking.

Our winters were very mild for many years, so cattle lived on the wild grass instead of being fed by the settlers. My father expected the mild weather to continue, but there came a bad winter with deep snow and the cattle he had bought with the mortgage money stood out in the weather without enough food. They became so poor and weak that some of them died. Others, when they went to the creek to drink, fell down and were unable to get up again. There they remained, perishing in the mud.

Then came a year when the grasshoppers ate the corn down to the ground. Another year there was not enough rain for the crops to develop. The dry winds blew, the wind was full of dust, and people were hungry.

The U.S. government sent us dry beans and pork fat. I have a letter that my father wrote to his brother back in Ohio asking for yarn so that mother could knit for the growing family. He specified that his brother was *not* to send any beans!

When the preacher came to our house, Mother always boiled a chicken. We children had to wait until the older folks were through eating, then all that was left was the neck, the back, and the ribs. You can imagine how we felt to see the preacher come.

My mother regularly cut a piece of rind from the pork, ran a string through it, and hanged it in the cupboard so she would have it to grease the griddle to keep pancakes from sticking. One day Aunt Addie, Uncle Will's wife, came to spend the day and when Mother went to the cupboard to get her "greaser," as she called it, it was nowhere to be found. Finally, Mother said, "Well, Addie, I do not know what to do. I can't find my greaser to grease the griddle for the pancakes." Aunt Addie said, "Oh, Ellen, I ate it." People were that hungry.

In dry seasons we sometimes had dried apples, though months often passed with no fruit. Our neighbors, the Longneckers, once received a barrel of apples from their people in Kentucky. We were there spending the day and Mrs. Longnecker gave each of us children an apple. Later in the day I decided I'd like another apple. Owens, one of their sons, and I were out in the yard playing, and the apples were in the cellar. I knew better than to steal one, so I persuaded Owens to go down and get one for me. He was coming up out of the cellar when his mother came out of the house and said, "Owens, what are you doing?" Owens replied, "Mary wanted an apple and I was getting it for her." She looked at me and then said, "That is all right, Mary, but you know Owens is not allowed to go down there without permission." As young as I was, I understood the polite reprimand, and felt ashamed that I had not acted like a lady.

Many incidents occurred in my earliest years and I still remember some going back as far as 1876, when I was three years old. Not knowing the seeds were poisonous, my mother allowed me to play with "Jimson" pods (stramonium). The pods containing the seeds rattled as I shook them, but some of them rattled out and I ate about a thimbleful. My mother said I came staggering to her and wanted to be taken, but she was busy and told me to go away and play. As I started away she noticed that something was wrong, so she caught me up and I clutched her hair.

Just then my father came in, took me in his arms, and I caught my hands in his whiskers. Mother gave me something to make me throw up, then she gave me cream and egg white and sent for the doctor. The doctor stayed all night and never left the crib, for I was deeply unconscious until late the next day when I began to recover.

In those years we could still see the marks of the great buffalo herds that traveled north in the spring and south in the fall as they followed the growing grass. They cut deep ruts in the sandy soil. We often walked in them or stepped across them on our way to school.

Also on the prairies were great buffalo wallows sometimes as much as two feet deep and from one hundred to two hundred feet across. In wet seasons they stood full of water. Rushes grew in them and we could hear the frogs croaking.

One day a buffalo came over the hill on his way to the creek to get a drink. We ran to the house and watched him through the window. He carried his head low and swung it from side to side as he walked. Another buffalo took up abode with our neighbor's cattle. He was a very gentle fellow and I remember that my father put me on his back as he lay there in the corral with the milk cows.

There were many coyotes, and here and there the little prairie dog had its community. A small owl seemed to live among them, as well as rattlesnakes.

Natural history folklore about animals living among prairie dogs abounded in the Midwest. Although many people thought that rattlesnakes and prairie dogs lived together, Lewis and Clark observed that rattlesnakes lived separately from prairie dogs in abandoned burrows.

Mother was forever warning us to be careful of rattlesnakes. A rattler bit one of the Loomis boys and he died. Another bit my Uncle Joe Crockford on the thumb, but my grandmother killed two chickens and applied the flesh to the wound. As fast as the chicken flesh turned green, she applied fresh. My uncle was very sick, but he recovered.

By about April first every year we were going barefoot. It was still pretty cold, especially in the mornings, but we thought it great fun to go barefoot. It was also economical, as it saved shoe leather. We herded the cattle to keep them out of the cornfields because there were few fences. After barbed wire was introduced, cattle and horses got terribly cut up until they learned to stay away from it.

There were two years between my sister Ida and me. I was the oldest. We often played together around the creek and used to kill frogs for fish bait. One day we were having no luck fishing and were looking for something else to do when we saw something make the grass wave. We soon discovered a skunk and right away decided to kill it, skin it, and sell the hide to make some money for ourselves. We threw sticks at it until it ran into the creek. While Ida went to gather more sticks to pelt it, I threw sticks and clods to keep it from climbing the other bank. Suddenly, it came up the bank right at my feet. I had only a little short stick in my hand but I whacked it on the head as hard as I could. Meanwhile, Ida came with more sticks and together we finally killed it, but by then we were well-scented.

We decided right there that we did not need any money. And we had had plenty of skunk. We hated to go home for we didn't know what Mother would say. She discovered us before we got into the house and came out saying, "Girls, for goodness' sake, what have you been doing now?" Poor Mother, she made us go to the barn and wait for her to bring clothes. It took a long time to get the odor out of our clothes.

At night Mother made us undress standing on a chair, then we stepped over onto the bed and put on our gowns. That way we avoided taking any fleas to bed. One night I went to stay all night with my cousin Myrtle Crockford and my aunt made us a bed on the floor as they didn't have enough bedsteads. The fleas tortured me and I made such a disturbance about the fleas that finally my aunt said, "Now Mary, you can see that fleas don't keep Myrtle awake, so you just make up your mind to go to sleep." Then I said, "Well, Myrtle is used to them and I'm not." I fussed around until four o'clock in the morning when I got up, dressed, and went alone the two miles home. I had to cross Red Willow Creek on a fallen tree. When I entered our house, Mother rose up in bed and said, "Mary, for goodness' sake, why are you home this time of day?" I was seven.

My father called me "Mary Lady, Sizzie Lizzie, Rose-Bud," until one day when I stole my sister May's earrings from a small oblong pillbox. May missed her earrings right away and I helped hunt for them. Finally, someone noticed that I was holding my hand over my pocket and they wanted to know what I had in it. I ran outdoors and sister May after me. When I saw she was going to catch me I threw the earrings as far as I could out into the weeds. No one found them, but my father added a new name to my pet name and I became "Mary Lady, Sizzie Lizzie, Rose-Bud, Pillbox." The pet name therefore became a name of reproach.

Our sod house was in the form of an el. The living room and kitchen ran north and south. Extending west from the kitchen was a shed that connected to the milkhouse. Under the shed was the hand-dug well, thirty feet deep with dirt walls. My father had built a curb around it. A rope with a bucket at the end ran through a grooved wheel and fastened to the ceiling of the shed. We children always played about the well because it was shady there; therefore we frequently dropped knives, forks, spoons, tin cups, and "what not" into the well until Mother said she didn't have enough left for her table. Someone would then have to go down and fish everything out.

Johnny Canaga, a cousin who lived with us, said that my brother Ben should go down because he was the only boy in our family. Ben didn't want to go, but Johnny kept calling him a coward until Ben finally said he would go. He put one foot into the well bucket and caught hold of the rope. As his head went down below the curb, however, he began to look terrified and screamed for Johnny to pull him up. "Pull me up, pull me up!" he kept screaming until Mother was afraid that in his terror he might tumble down anyway. So Johnny drew him up and lifted him out of the bucket. Mother said, "Well, how are we going to get the things out of the well?" I thought about it a little while and then said, "I'll go."

Now, I was nine years old and Ben was ten. Mother said, "Mary, do you want to go?" I said, "Yes, I'll go." I put one foot into the bucket and held onto the rope and as my head began to go down I understood what scared Ben so. I didn't say anything, but I looked sharp to see if there might be a snake or something peeping out from a hole in the wall. It was cool and dark as I descended. At long last I came to the water. It seemed ice-cold and it came up to my hips so that I couldn't stoop over to pick anything up. I felt around with my feet and got each thing between my toes. One at a time I put them in the bucket. Then they pulled the articles up while I waited for the bucket to come back down for me. Mother called out from above, "Mary, be careful the bucket don't hit your head!" I made no demonstration of fear, but when I got my feet on the ground again I felt a great relief.

There were short fat worms that lived in the manure pile and we used to dig them out for fish bait. One day I found quite a few and put them in a can. I ran to the house and poured them all out in Mother's lap as she sat in a chair sewing. She didn't have the same idea I had about those worms, and when she saw them in her lap she screamed, jumped up, and threw them all over the floor. I was astonished because they were harmless.

In wet seasons we waded in the lowlands where the rushes grew, and often found frog eggs. From day to day we watched them hatch, grow into tadpoles, and then real frogs. I used to play with an old fat toad and Mother said that it was the cause of my warts, but I couldn't believe it because Mother had a wart on her finger and she never touched them.

One winter day my sister May said to my mother that she wanted to scare Ida and me. Ida and I were playing upstairs. Mother entered the scheme and dressed May in men's clothes, then fixed up a big bundle of clothes for her to carry, and sent her outdoors.

Mother called us to come downstairs at once as there was a tramp coming and May was in the barn. She said one of us must go down and get her. We came downstairs and when we looked out, there was the tramp just climbing through the fence with a bundle so large he could hardly get it under the fence. I said I would go to the barn to get May and started out hippity-hopping so the tramp wouldn't think I was afraid of him.

When I was about halfway to the barn I looked back and to my terror the tramp was coming after me. Of course, I started to run round and round the barn, dodging the tramp, and calling for May at every jump. I thought of taking off for the timber where I could hide, but then I thought he could track me as there was an inch or two of snow on the ground. At last, the tramp turned and met me head-on. By then May was laughing so hard she fell down in the snow and I on top of her. I enjoyed the joke as much as the rest when I understood it.

Uncle Will and Aunt Addie lived up on the high divide and one year, after they thrashed their wheat, they had a wonderful stack of clean straw. Mother took us all there to sleep in the straw stack. Uncle Will, Aunt Addie, and their four children, together with Mother and her five, all slept in that sweet-smelling straw. My father did not do such "silly" things, but we thought it was wonderful. I remember looking up at that wondrous dome of heaven and seeing shooting stars and the great Milky Way streaming across the wide world above. I wondered, "If the world ends, will the stars all come tumbling down?" Our older folks often talked of the world ending. I often worried about that, especially while Mother was in town. I feared it would happen while she was away and I wouldn't know what in the world to do.

All of us children relied upon and enjoyed Mother, but there were occasional disagreements. It was Mother's idea for me to wash the dishes and for sister Ida to wipe them, she being two years younger. One morning I took a notion that it was about time for Ida to wash them and for me to wipe them. My mother was not a patient woman, and when she told us to do something she expected it done. That was in the days when the rod was not spared.

I said, "Ida can wash them." Mother said, "Mary, you go and wash the dishes." I said, "Ida can do them. It's not fair for me to wash them all the time." Mother said, "Mary, if you don't get at the dishes, I'll whip you." Again I repeated that Ida could do them.

Mother kept some willow whips for insubordinations and here was rebellion in the raw. She began to whip me and she laid it on until she wore the whip out. Then she got another one and began on me with that too, striking me across the back. My clothes were thin, the pain was almost unbearable, and *it would have been* if I hadn't felt the injustice of it. A great feeling of rage took possession of me and I do believe Mother might have killed me before I gave in to such punishment. By the time she had worn the third whip out, she was herself exhausted and sat down and began to cry. Then I melted and went over to the table and washed the dishes.

Mary's daughter Nellie once told how, when she was a girl in Lebanon, Oregon, a neighbor told Mary a lie about Nellie. Mary believed the neighbor against Nellie's protestations and took her upstairs to spank her with a hairbrush. As it was her tenth birthday, Nellie asked Mary to stop at ten. "But," said Nellie, "I remember counting to seventeen."

Mother never forced an issue with me again. I know she worried a lot about me because I was willful. I was determined never to be "bossed." If a thing was right for me to do, I would do it, but it must seem right for me. I would make myself do the right thing without being shoved around by anyone. My mother loved her children, but she was a dominating person and sometimes had bad judgment. But there was never a sacrifice she was unwilling to make for one of her children in need.

One early morning Mother and I went down to the meadow to see if the wild plums were ripe. There was a thicket of them on the other side of our meadow. It had rained the night before and the grass was dripping with moisture. We were both barefoot and as we waded through the grass we held our dresses up out of the moisture. I was a little way ahead of Mother when suddenly she screamed, "Mary, there's a snake around your leg." I didn't look to see which leg, but jumped into the air and ran a block or two before I stopped. Somewhere along the way I lost the snake. Mother said afterwards she thought it must have been a garter snake.

One of our neighbors found the skeleton of an Indian in the crotch of an old cottonwood tree. We children used to go there to hunt for the beads that fell on the ground as the Indian's clothes decayed. We found beads in anthills several hundred yards away.

News went by word of mouth and anything that happened of real significance was soon over a large part of the state. East of us a farmer was thrashing wheat with an old horse-powered machine as was the custom. A man and boy were cutting the bundles and feeding them into the machine. The boy accidentally cut the man's hand, and it so enraged him that he picked the boy up and fed him into the machine. When the other men working at the place understood what the man had done, they unhitched the horses, elevated a wagon tongue, and strung the man up right there.

East of our neighborhood a man fell in love with a married woman. I never heard how long the affair had been going on, but finally the man offered the woman's husband three hundred dollars for her. The husband, after thinking it over, decided he could do more with three hundred dollars than an unwilling wife, so a divorce was given. The woman became the wife of the other man and they came to our neighborhood to live. As a child I used to look at her and wonder what it was that made her worth so much money. She seemed very ordinary to me. Three hundred dollars was a vast sum in those days.

One neighbor woman took a horse team out after her husband warned her they couldn't be trusted. She put her four children into the wagon after hitching it up, then drove off to look for wild plums. A tumbleweed scared the horses and they ran away. She was unable to control them and they upset the wagon, killing one of her children. The other children weren't badly injured.

When we lived by the creek, my mother was sick all one fall and winter. She had grown so anemic and pale that she looked dead. We didn't know what the trouble was, but every three days she had chills and a high temperature, then she perspired freely and felt better for another three days. When she chilled I built a big fire in the stove and piled the bedcovers over her, which never seemed enough to warm her. After she suffered all that time, my father took her to the doctor who gave her quinine. He said she had ague, which is usually malarial. I have often thought about that, wishing I had known then what caused her sickness and what to do for her. A few capsules of quinine cured her.

My mother didn't tell her children fairy tales to put them to sleep at night, but instead experiences from her own childhood. The stories were very simple but always amusing to us. When she was sixteen and very shy, she was on her way along a timbered trail in Gratiot County, Michigan. At the time, bears were plentiful in Michigan's heavy timber. A man was sawing wood by the trail and Mother thought to pass behind him so she wouldn't need to speak. She left the trail to circle around, and when she was directly behind him she accidentally stepped on a stick. It broke with a loud report and the man—thinking the noise was a bear—jumped and screamed loudly. This scared Mother and she also gave out a loud scream. There they stood screaming at each other. The man apologized after he saw her, saying he thought a bear had sneaked up on him.

Another time, Mother's parents left her alone in their log house with her two brothers, William and Jacob. She was only twelve, and her two brothers were sixteen and two, respectively. She was cooking in the fireplace in the evening when they decided to bring in the dog to play. To prevent Jake from falling into the fireplace, they cut two holes in a gunny sack, put his legs through them, and hung him up on a wooden peg where he could watch the fun. They decided to put the cowbell on the dog and see what he would do. It scared the dog and he ran round and round the room, whining and trying to shake the thing off. Finally, he jumped through the open window and ran down into the swamp, the bell

jingling, jangling all the way. Soon they couldn't hear it
anymore. Mother and Will looked at each other in as-
tonishment, then Will pointed a finger at Mother and
said, "Ellen, you'll catch it when the folks get home
and find that bell lost." They never found the bell, but
the dog finally came home.

The old log schoolhouse we attended was once a
home for earlier pioneers. It was on the road that led
covered wagon traffic westward along the Republican
River. Sitting barefoot at the window, I often counted
fifty wagons a day going slowly by. I used to wonder
how big *the West* must be to take care of that great
migration, so many human beings seeking homes and
freedom.

One day at school I got hurt and was leaning against
the school building crying when a boy named Lon came
up and said, "Cry baby! Cry baby!" At that I gave him
a big shove and he fell backwards into the sand burrs.
He went bawling to the teacher who came out and
wanted to know what it was all about. One of the older
boys came up and said he'd seen the whole thing, that
I got hurt and cried and Lon called me a cry baby. He
said that I then shoved Lon and he fell into the sand
burrs. The teacher said to Lon, "It was good enough for
you!" Of course, I felt justified, but my brother Ben and
sister May took the news home to Mother who told me
I better not fight anymore.

Not long after that I was walking home from school
with another girl who lived nearby, and a boy followed
us teasing the girl, pulling her braids, and doing other
abusive things to her. At last, I said to the girl, "I
wouldn't take that." Then the boy said, "You're the one
I mean." I forgot all about Mother's telling me not to

fight, turned on the boy, and gave him a good shove. He fell right across a buffalo rut. He let us alone after that, but my brother Ben and sister May hightailed it for home to tell Mother that "Mary was fighting again."

When I got home Mother gave me a good switching and then went to see the chairman of the school board, Mr. Buck. When Mother told her tale, Mr. Buck said, "Now, Mrs. Canaga, you let Mary alone. She is defending herself." Mother came home feeling sorry that she had punished me.

Another year, when my brother Ben and I entered school, the teacher said to my brother, "What kind of boy are you?" Ben said, "Well, I'm a holy terror." The teacher said, "Very well, Sir, I'll put you in the back seat with Stella Peak and I'll expect you to behave yourself." Ben did pretty well for a few days, but one day when he started to the front for a class recitation, Stella Peak started to race him. They were both on a fast run when they got to the front seats. Then the teacher said, "Now Sir, don't let that happen again." Ben replied, "Well, Stella tried to race me, and I just forgot I was in the school room."

At Christmas there was always a Christmas tree at the schoolhouse. While not always an evergreen, it was beautiful with candles, strings of popcorn and cranberries, and presents for all the children. For each of the children there was always a bag of candy and nuts (mostly peanuts), a popcorn ball, and an apple. Luckily, there was never a disaster with the lit candles and wads of cotton swabbing that represented snow around the tree. I don't even think people considered the fire and tinder dangerous at the time.

We went to the schoolhouse in the winter, covered

ts and blankets, riding in our lumber wagon
g on hay in the wagon box. It was plenty cold
and the wheels squeaked over the snow.

Entertainment on the Nebraska prairie included
weekly meetings or ice cream socials at church, and
"literary society" gatherings, public interest debates, or
spelling bees at the schoolhouse. At home our books included a Christian bible and my father's geography and
astronomy texts. My neighbor Kate Longnecker and I
spent many nights studying the astronomy book and
finding constellations in the heavens.

Occasionally, there were recitations and "singing
bees" to vary the entertainment. I always read from my
favorite stories: *John Maynard*, *Briar Rose*, or *The
Sharp Trade*. I enjoyed getting up before people and
showing off. I was very dramatic.

The first story that I ever read—I was thirteen—was
from the Red Willow County newspaper that came into
our house wrapped around something. After reading the
story, it became my sole object in life to read everything I could lay my hands on. I borrowed books or
magazines from all the neighbors. One lent me a great
pile of *New York Ledgers*, silly romances, but at the
time I was unable to distinguish between slush and clas-
sical literature. I was always reading, but didn't hear of
Shakespeare, Dickens, or even James Fenimore Cooper
until I was sixteen.

My constant reading irritated Mother, who wanted
me to work. She threatened me with dire ends if I didn't
stop. She threatened to buy me the *Police Gazette*, as it
was the worst bit of reading material she could imagine
and thought it might frighten me.

I was growing up and I made up my mind that I was

going to get more learning than our country school offered. I went to the town of Indianola to go to school and found a place where I could work for my room and board. My teacher took an interest in me at once and began to direct my reading.

The first really good book I ever read was Dickens' *Oliver Twist*. Also that first winter, along with my schoolwork, I read the *Leatherstocking Tales* of Cooper and Daniel Defoe's *Robinson Crusoe*.

Soon I began to read only what I regarded as books of substance. I also studied English grammar carefully, as I was reticent to converse with people for fear of making errors.

A Teacher Named Walter

I learned grammar well enough to teach at a little country school twenty miles from Goodland, Kansas. There I stayed with my grandmother. There were only three months in the fall term. After Christmas I went back to school in Indianola, Nebraska, where I had a new teacher: J. Walter Rowland. Mr. Rowland was of small bones, dark hair, and dark blue eyes, with that wit and ready answer that go with the Irish.

Mr. Rowland's wife had died of an obstruction of the bowels. In those days, there were no local care facilities to handle such cases. The youngest of his four children was four months old when his wife died. Mr. Rowland's mother took the baby, John, to care for him, but the other three stayed with him and went to school with me.

I roomed alone while in school in Indianola. One day a woman, Mrs. Ryder, came to visit and begged me to let her daughter May stay with me. She said the family May roomed with made her work so hard for her board that she had no time to study. I knew her daughter from school and she seemed aristocratic. The poor woman cried and suggested I try May as a roommate for one month, then if I didn't like her she would go back to the other home. This was the beginning of one of my dearest friendships. May came to live with me for the school year.

May Ryder was small and dainty, with light hair and brown eyes. Her memory is dear to me, though I have not seen her these many years. During the winter when we stayed together in Indianola, there came to our local opera house a medicine vaudeville show called the Kickapoo Indian Show. On the last night of the show, a set of silverware was to be given to the most beautiful girl in the audience.

On weeknights the company had a large crowd, but on Saturday night people from far and wide packed into the show. Everybody in the community was restless for entertainment. The skilled snake oil barker persuaded many to buy bottles of the medicine show's miracle concoction. I imagine it had a high percentage of alcohol to provide a needed *lift*. The barker recommended it as having great virtue for all complaints.

Although I was ill on the last night with tonsillitis, I persuaded May to go, for I thought she was the most beautiful girl anywhere. At about ten o'clock I heard her running on the wooden sidewalk and with every step she was calling, "O, Mary, I got the silverware, I got it, I got it." The dear child! She said, "A big Indian came down the aisle; he stopped and looked at me, then went on to the back of the hall. When he came back, he stopped again. I was so embarrassed I just covered my face with my fan. He went up front and said he'd found the most beautiful girl, then he indicated me and brought over the silverware."

The next day Old Envy showed up. One girl remarked, "He never saw me." Another said, "I might have had it if I had put a barrel of flour on my face."

In the autumn Walter began to pay attention to me. Often he came to our apartment where we read together while May studied. We read *Evangeline*, *Song of Hiawatha*, *The Courtship of Miles Standish*, *Lucile*, and *Ivanhoe*; also some of Dickens' works. Occasionally he suggested that I would be happy as his wife, but at the time I wanted to be a missionary and my thoughts carried me off into the land of spirituality. I had never thought of living for myself.

As time passed I grew to love him, notwithstanding the difference in our ages. No other man ever moved my emotions like Walter.

Walter was almost fifteen years older than Mary.

Meanwhile, I was in school for a purpose, was diligent in my studies, and made good grades. At this time, another girl in my class tried to create Walter's interest. She stayed after school and pretended she didn't understand the problems and needed extra help. Between her, her sister, and mother they stirred up much feeling against me, calling me the teacher's pet behind my back.

Walter was not happy teaching because he disliked disciplining the children. His first marriage took place when he was very young, in Ohio. He had left his wife and two children with his family in Ohio to go to Kansas where he worked his way through Kansas Normal College at Fort Scott. Then he studied both telegraphy and law. He passed the Nebraska state bar, but law did not suit him either.

According to Walter's application for a certificate from the Kansas State Board of Medical Registration

*and Examination, the Kansas City Medical College
of Missouri admitted him to the second year class on
presentation of his normal college diploma.*

Always with a family to support, he fell back on teaching. He had four children when his wife died. He was
not physically very strong, but had a fine mind. One of
his friends advised him to study medicine because he
seemed more like a doctor than anything else. He finally decided and prepared to go away to medical
school. After I began teaching regularly, I loaned him
every cent I could spare. It was tough going for him for
a long time.

When Walter left, a new teacher, Mr. Smith, replaced
him. I studied as diligently as ever, but it was soon apparent that someone had influenced him against me. Besides teaching the classes of the high school, Mr. Smith
was superintendent of the entire school.

Such an atmosphere of frigidity developed toward me
that I would have dropped out if I had not wanted to
learn. The students were quite determined that I should
not become the teacher's pet again. I was noticeably ignored in classes.

Finally, the county superintendent of schools heard
about the situation and paid the school a visit. I told
him the struggle I had to keep myself in school. He
knew how hard I had worked for my board those first
years and how I had taught in the hot summers to earn
money to continue school during the winter months.

After the visit, Mr. Smith turned it all over in his
mind and one day he came to my desk before the entire
high school and said, "Miss Canaga, I owe you an apol-

ogy for treating you as I have. I have been laboring under a misunderstanding about you and I am very, very sorry."

I was so embarrassed I could have crawled under my desk, but glad too to think the atmosphere would be better now. The girl, the mother, and sister who created the negative atmosphere for me are now dead many years. If only people could realize how futile envy and jealousy are. Life goes on and to harbor such unworthy thoughts only creates unhappiness. In the language of the immortal Shakespeare in *Othello*,

"Good name in man and woman, dear my Lord,
Is the immediate jewel of their souls;
Who steals my purse steals trash;
    'tis something, nothing;
'twas mine, 'tis his, and has been slave to thousands;
But he that filches from me my good name
Robs me of that which not enriches him,
And makes me poor indeed."

About this time, my mother's only sister wrote to ask if I would come to Iowa where they lived and help get ready for my cousin's wedding. If I came, she said she'd give me money for the teachers' institute and I could teach at their school.

When the time came for me to go to the institute, however, my uncle said he didn't have the money. Another uncle said he knew a young man who would loan me the money if I would ask him for it. I made the request and borrowed the money, then paid him back with my first check. My aunt wanted me to board with her, but I was unable to get along with her husband; consequently, I stayed with a neighbor for the rest of the term.

The county superintendent in Iowa, a woman, was very arrogant toward out-of-state teachers since she felt Iowa had "too many teachers already." She marked me as low in my grades as she could, but gave me a certificate to teach in the county.

I gained a valuable lesson from this experience, for I made the vow then that if the time ever came that I had authority over other people I wouldn't behave in a domineering manner. I have never liked the "Big I, Little You" idea. The finest people in this world are the most unassuming, and I have always taught my little daughter: "Be somebody and you do not have to put it on." The experience also reminded me of what Job said to the people who told him to curse God: "No doubt you are the people and wisdom will die with you."

After Walter graduated in medicine, he didn't have enough money to buy office equipment. He therefore took another school at Cedar Bluffs, Kansas. While teaching there, he heard that a doctor was needed a few miles west at a little town called Herndon.

He located there and for equipment bought a medicine case, a hypodermic, an obstetrical forceps, and a very good line of forceps for extracting teeth. In those days, a doctor had to do dental work (extracting, not filling teeth), otherwise it fell to the druggist. He had a fair medical library that he studied diligently. As fast as he made money practicing, he bought equipment, and soon he was doing very well.

After he had practiced for a year, I decided that if we were ever going to be married it was about time. We had been interested in each other for five years. We corresponded regularly when we were apart. I wrote him that I was ready to marry and if he was not interested there was a man nearer home I could love very easily.

His response surprised me. He raved, "That is just like a woman. You can set all your hopes on her for a lifetime, and then suddenly she goes off after someone else." I answered him that we had waited a long time. I had been going out some with Owens Longnecker who was a fine young man, one of the best. I thought there should be a time limit.

Right away he wrote that he had purchased a little house in Herndon and for me to fix a time. On May 23, 1897, I married my beloved man in my mother's home and went to live in Herndon, Kansas. When he came to the wedding, he gave me a deed to the house he had just purchased and remarked that it was better than a diamond ring.

Life in Herndon

Herndon, Kansas, with a population of about three hundred, was located along the lightly timbered banks of Beaver Creek. There were Hungarian, Bohemian, Irish, and largely German immigrants, and south of the main part of town a settlement of Swedes. German was the prevailing language among these groups, though most of the population of Herndon spoke English. There were Roman Catholic, Lutheran, and German Congregational churches in the community.

This was my first association with foreigners, whose manners and customs were so different from those of my family. The women routinely wore shawls over their heads as women today do in stormy weather. They wore half a dozen skirts at once. But while their appearance was queer, they were always friendly. Women came to visit me and sat in my house smiling, for in speaking we could not understand each other. In time I learned much German.

As a little girl, Mary's daughter Nellie described seeing a German man trying to express his medical problem. Standing in Mary's waiting room, he pointed to various parts of his body and said, "Hurt me here. Hurt me here. Hurt me here."

The only differences between these recent immigrants' ancestors and my own ancestors were that mine had come to America two hundred years before and were here to fight in the Revolutionary War. My ancestors helped make America what it became for all newcomers. I soon learned that these people, having followed the dream only later, were just as worthy as my own family.

At one time Mary applied for membership in the Daughters of the American Revolution, was accepted, then declined to join when she discovered she disagreed with DAR political views. On her father's side of the family, Mary was descendent to Susannah Livingston (1780–1830), daughter of Christian Livingston, a Revolutionary War soldier who fought under General Washington. Christian Livingston died in 1813.

The German Congregational Church conducted services in English and it was there that I attended and worked fervently until one day Dr. Rowland said he did not think it was necessary to "go to seed" on religion. I thought about that idea a lot and it modified my ideas and made me less of a zealot.

When my husband—and I later—began to practice medicine in northwestern Kansas, we were about halfway between Kansas City and Denver where the nearest hospitals were, three or four hundred miles away. At times we sent patients to Kansas City if it happened that major surgery was necessary, but for the most part we took care of them in homes or at our office, with no help except from family members. There were no dentists except the doctor or the barber.

The Doctor had a very unfortunate experience in his practice a short while before we were married. It disturbed him so much that he was ready to quit the practice of medicine. A young woman who had been in labor three days finally sent for him. When he arrived, an arm was protruding and the woman was completely ensanguinated. These days people consult doctors who do Caesarean section and can take the baby through the abdomen.

Doctor had no help except the family, but he was able to turn the baby and remove it. It was already dead and the mother died within half an hour. His arrival was too late to save either, but that, of course, was not his fault. Those ignorant people thought he had killed her and he vowed he would never take a confinement case again. He said they never sent for a doctor until something was dead wrong and then expected the doctor to do a miracle. They had waited until the hand was born and until the mother had hemorrhaged to the limit before they sent for him. She was in a dying condition when he arrived, but he thought he might save the baby, which proved futile.

One night early in the evening a German man came and called for the Doctor. He said, "My vife vants to make a baby and she vants you to help." Doctor said, "How long has she been sick?" He replied, "Oh, two days." Doctor said, "I won't go a step; if you can't send for me right away I will not go and then get the blame if it doesn't go right." I didn't know the first thing about delivering a baby, but I knew he couldn't practice medicine in a country community and not take his cases as they came. I got out of bed and said, "Yes, you will. I'll go with you." After that I always went with him for moral support.

It was a fortunate thing for me that I could bury myself in Doctor's medical books. I wanted to understand everything so that I might be of help to him. How wonderful to study the human body, its physical makeup, the why and where of each part and its function; to study how to tell one ailment from another, the best forms of treatment, and how the baby develops in the mother.

My thoughts always went back to the time when I was a child and parents told their children tales of how babies came into homes. Mother had a good story of how she found each one of us, and how I told a bachelor, after I was twelve years old, that Mother found me in a prairie dog's hole. How embarrassed the bachelor and Mother had acted. I said, "Well, you did, didn't you?" After the bachelor left, Mother told me different. People used to think the Lord must have done a dirty job when he created a human being. Everything was certainly Under Cover.

Many of the immigrants around Herndon slept between two feather beds, and it was the custom in those days to deliver a woman without having her uncovered. They told me of a doctor who, at the last minute before the baby came, threw the top feather tick off. Such shameful exposure; they would never have that doctor again! How the world has changed.

The birth of a baby is a most wonderful episode. When the time is ripe, there is a complicated mechanism set in motion, and there is no stopping it until a new life comes into this world to go through development to youth, maturity, death, and decay. The baby is squeezed into the birth canal, usually head first. Down it goes and the pressures turn it this way and that to conform to the canal. Slowly the uterus contracts and the lower parts dilate until the head is born, then there is a half-turn to allow the shoulders through. How did people ever think there was anything but something wonderful in all of this? It seems to me simply miraculous.

At first Doctor drove an old nag, but one evening he came home with a beautiful, dappled gray horse. He said he had traded his nag for the horse. The farmer who owned the horse said he was too high-lifed to hitch to a plow, and gave ten dollars extra to get rid of him.

The very next night, Doctor hitched up "Prince" and went away on a professional call, but when he came home his nerves were shot to pieces and he was on the verge of hysteria. He said, "In the morning I'm going to take that horse out and shoot him. He ran all the way back to the farmer's where I bought him and I could no more hold him than I could hold the wind. Then when I got him started back here he took off and ran all the way back. I'll shoot him if it's the last thing I do!"

Doctor couldn't sleep, but kept up a continual muttering about shooting the horse. Later in the night he said, "I know what I'll do. I'll sell him. I'll sell him if I only get ten dollars." About midnight he said, "I know what I'll do, I'll put a J.I.C. bit on him." This bit was hinged in the middle so that when someone pulled the reins it pinched the horse's mouth. Doctor put the bit on the horse and it proved to be a good idea. In time I grew very fond of Prince.

I spent all my spare time studying Doctor's medical books and after we were married a year, out of a clear sky, Doctor said to me, "How would you like to study medicine in earnest?" I said, "Oh, I would if I could." Then he said, "Well, if you want, I am going to send you through medicine." It wouldn't be in my power to express the gratitude I felt for what he proposed to do for me. He said, "It will be a fine arrangement for us to practice together."

There was a small medical school in Topeka, Kansas, which later consolidated with Kansas City Medical. I went to this school in the fall and tried to commit everything to memory so that my husband shouldn't think I was wasting his money. The Doctor's oldest daughter was married, and his oldest son and younger daughter kept house in Herndon with him. I didn't realize at the time how much of a sacrifice it was to him to have me gone from our home. I was so full of ambition to learn that I didn't even think how it was for them. I went away to study medicine because my husband wanted me to and because I was absorbed in learning about the human body.

Many elements went into my development as a mature woman. My father always said his girls were just as smart as his boy, and my husband said I was as capable as any man. In the medical college at Topeka, the boys at the college treated the girls as pals. We studied and quizzed together. All these ideas made me believe in myself and made me think I could do something worthwhile in the world.

After our first examination at school, one of the men

at the college told me that someone wanted to talk with me on the phone. Phones were new at the time and I had never before talked on one. I didn't know anyone in Topeka except those associated with the college. I thought they were fooling me and I didn't want to go out into the hall where the phone was. But the young man persisted, saying that someone really wanted to talk with me, so I finally went.

A man's voice said, "Is this Mrs. Rowland?" I said, "Yes, who are you?" The voice said, "I'm a friend of yours, don't you remember we were out together the other night?" Then I said, "I haven't been anywhere." It occurred to me that someone had gotten the wrong person on the phone. I said, "Who is it you want to talk to?" Again the voice said, "Why, you are Mrs. Rowland, aren't you?" Then he said, "I can't hear a word you say." Then I said, "Well, Sir, I'm not talking." Then I heard him laugh and I asked, "Are you the Doctor?" He came back with, "I'm *a* doctor." Then it began to dawn on me that it was my Doctor.

He asked, "What did you get in chemistry?" I said, "Well, I got one hundred percent, but I want to know where you are." He had slipped away to come down to see me and was near the school. We went to Kansas City for the weekend and visited another physician and his wife. The physician had allowed my husband to sleep on a couch in his office while he was studying medicine and we felt very grateful to him.

At the Christmas vacation on my way home I went as far as Dresden, Kansas, on the Rock Island Railroad. There Doctor met me. We had Christmas dinner with relatives of his and then drove to Herndon, arriving about midnight. We had just lit the lamp when a neighbor came to tell us that his brother had, a few hours before, shot himself to death.

Udo was one of three brothers who owned a flour mill. He had been suffering from delusions and thought everybody was making fun of him. He had come to consult Doctor several weeks before and while conversing suddenly caught Doctor by the throat and said, "Are you making fun of me?" Of course, he should have been put in an asylum at once, but his brothers wanted him treated at home.

In the meantime, Udo thought he would go to the asylum by himself so he got on the train and started. When he got part way there he turned back home saying that so many people were making fun of him that he was afraid he would kill someone. It seems strange that his family allowed him to go about by himself. I suppose some people allow a member of the family to have their freedom even when they know it may be unsafe. Insanity is a disease of the brain and many cases are curable if treated.

On Christmas day, Udo and his wife had dinner with his brother Louie and afterwards he and his brother played checkers. Then Udo said he would go home and take a nap, and his wife insisted on going with him. They lived in the outskirts of town, and when they got home Udo lay down on the bed and told his wife she could let him sleep. She went into the other room and was standing in front of the mirror fixing her hair when she heard a tremendous report. She ran to his door and found it locked. She ran around to look in the window and saw him there dead, then ran out to the road and called for the neighbors who came right away.

After his family told us of the tragedy, I went into the

kitchen and felt very queer, then I thought that I'd go and tell Doctor that I didn't feel well. I fell in the doorway in a dead faint. Udo's folks said they would rather have him dead than in an asylum. I know people used to think there was some disgrace about insanity. In ancient times, insane persons were persecuted and mistreated, and often driven from their homes and left to wander. People thought they were possessed of the Devil. People always have an answer for everything whether they understand it or not.

The next summer during the hot weather, an old gentleman tried to commit suicide. He succeeded in cutting through the trachea but failed to cut the carotid artery, the jugular vein, or the pneumogastric nerve. It was some fifteen miles there and Doctor went out, sewed up his throat, and left a stomach tube with instructions on how to feed him through it. The old man was getting along fine, but his neighbors decided that if he should die his soul ought to be taken care of. They took him to a dirty pool of water and went through the ceremony of baptism. The water from the pool infected the wound and he died.

For compensation, Doctor took a little mare. She was flea-bitten and very willing, but it developed that she was with foal and we turned her out to pasture. We called her "Lady." While Doctor was on a trip to Chicago, Lady gave birth to a mule colt. When he got back all the men in town who met him on the street held their arms up to their heads, waggled their fingers, and brayed. The men had their little joke about it. No one was more astonished than Doctor.

Dr. Rowland's great delight was to play tricks on me, as I was very credulous and believed everything he told me. One day he asked if I had ever seen a Limburger cheese, and I said no. I thought no more about it. Later on he slipped a piece of one in my pillow case. After we had gone to bed I smelled a dreadful odor. I began to talk about it and asked him, as I shook the bedclothes, if he had anything to do with it. He said he had not, but I thought I heard him laughing. Then he said he was not laughing. I decided that maybe it was the cat. I said, "If that cat has been under the bed I'll have it killed."

I climbed out of bed and made him hold the light while I tore the bed to pieces and raised the mattress up to have a good look. There was nothing there. We went back to bed, but I continued to smell that awful odor. About midnight I threw up and then he was sorry. He had no idea, he said, that it would make me sick. He said he was scared to death when I tore the bed to pieces for fear I'd give him the pillow with the Limburger cheese when I straightened it up again. I enjoyed the joke after I knew it.

When we visited the fair at Omaha, we visited the Cudahy Packing House. Doctor had gone to the restroom when I asked the man who was branding hams how many hams he branded each day. He said, "Oh, about one hundred thousand a day." Afterwards I was telling Doctor and he said, "Lord, woman, did you believe that?" I thought it was a great many hams, but I never doubted it. I laughed too then, to think how I'd been taken in.

I was reading a medical book and ran across the word "lentigo." I asked Doctor what it was and he said, "That is a disease I never saw and wouldn't be able to diagnose if I saw it." I looked it up and it said "freckles." How he laughed.

Our life together, however, was not all peaches and cream. Often, when he wasn't busy, he went downtown and loafed with the men, leaving me to entertain his two younger children together with the two children of our local druggist whose wife had died. I would tell them stories and they enjoyed listening, but it irked me to have to entertain four children, none of whom were really mine. I set myself to cure the Doctor of his habit. One night I disappeared and stayed away all night. The next morning when I came home he never said a word about it, but after that I had some cooperation. It was summertime and I had spent the night in the haymow. I had not gone to a neighbor's as it would have made talk. Doctor could play jokes on me, but he couldn't impose on me. One of my sisters said once that any man would impose on a woman if she let him, but I think it works both ways.

A woman once asked Doctor how his second wife compared to his first. He said that his first wife had been a better housekeeper but the second one was far superior mentally and he was having trouble keeping up. He always called me "The New Woman." New to him. In the nineteenth century women incubated many ideas that were new and opposed by many. People used to say, "Every man to his trade, but every woman to the washtub."

Before our marriage, a neighbor woman made the remark that if Doctor Rowland married that Mary Canaga he would marry a girl who couldn't even sew a button on. It is true that I didn't know very much about the things I was *supposed* to know about, such as house-keeping.

For a long time after we were married, Doctor called my biscuits "death balls." I don't believe I was worth three hundred dollars, the price the other man had paid for his woman, but then Doctor got me for nothing. I always liked to cook when I gave my attention to it. My father said I was the best cook in his family. My mother resented that and said if he would get her something to cook with she could cook too. Today I know women who have kept homes for years and still are unable to make good biscuits.

Doctor was telling me one day how much abuse his mother had taken from his father who drank: neglect, physical roughness, and humiliation, and all without a murmur. I flared up and said, "You would have thought just as much of her if she'd defended herself and stood up for her rights." She was such a fine, gentle soul, I do not know how anyone could have mistreated her. We have those creatures in this world. They never seem to protect themselves against the buffets of unkind fate. They always seem to draw to themselves some selfish brutes, for whom they nurture and care.

The Herndon hotel proprietor sat in the front of the hotel and collected money from customers while his wife cooked, washed dishes, cleaned, and made beds. He had the reputation of getting drunk and beating his wife. He knocked her down into the cellar once and broke some of her ribs and Doctor took care of her. When she recovered, she said her husband had never touched her. So much for loyalty. The hotel proprietor also owned the livery barn, which is now a thing of the past. It was a place where men loafed and made remarks as women passed.

In August, after the wheat was cut and stacked, ready for threshing, several brothers came to town with a threshing outfit. The older brother made a bargain with the hotel owner to stable the horses in his barn. The younger brother didn't understand what the bargain was and went into the barn to feed the horses. He was feeding them from the owner's grain when the owner came in and accused him of stealing. Apparently they were supposed to feed the horses with their own grain. It was all a misunderstanding, but there were a good many words said.

The next day across the street from the hotel in front of the post office the quarrel was taken up again. The hotel proprietor and his son were on one side and the two brothers on the other. According to witnesses, the proprietor and his son started the argument again. Words were exchanged until the proprietor called the older brother a liar. The brother then struck the proprietor, and his son whipped out a revolver and shot both of the brothers. The older brother dropped right where he stood and was carried across the street into the hotel. A couple of men brought the younger brother to our house for treatment, as he was wounded in the arm.

I think now that Doctor was more excited than anyone because the hotel proprietor had slandered him previously and he felt very resentful toward him. He asked if they had caught the murderer yet. Doctor told me to take care of the man who had come to our house and he went to the hotel to see if he could do anything for the older brother.

On examination, I found that the bullet had gone

through his forearm and between the bones without any fracture. After passing through the arm it had struck his suspender buckle, making a lump as large as an egg just below his heart. I gave him some medicine for shock and dressed his wound. He wanted to go back downtown to see if his brother was still alive. I went with him, as I was anxious about the situation and wondered what, if anything, Doctor could do for the older brother.

He was lying on a cot in the dining room of the hotel, having great difficulty breathing, for the bullet had penetrated his right lung, gone through his body, and lodged under the skin, barely missing the spine. As he labored to breathe, the air bubbled up from the bullet hole. Doctor said that if he survived the shock he would have a chance to live. There were no transfusions to stimulate recovery in those days.

He lingered for three weeks, the pleural cavity gradually filling with blood. When Doctor aspirated it, he removed a gallon of uncoagulated blood. He made a recovery, but the right lung was completely collapsed and useless. Some years afterwards he died of tuberculosis. The proprietor obtained a change of venue for the trial of his son and the jury cleared him. Many in the community thought it was a great miscarriage of justice, asking why the revolver had been so handy if he hadn't intended to use it. The son had the reputation of being wild and afterwards ran away from home. No one ever heard of him again, to the great grief of his mother.

Kansas was a prohibition state and had been for many years before I lived there, but the bootlegger had an occasional establishment called a "blind pig." The church people opposed them and tried in many ways to do away with them. In one neighborhood where one flourished, the preacher preached a long sermon against it and then prayed that the Lord would destroy it. Behold, lightning struck the building, burned it to the ground, and the owner sued the preacher for damages. The poor preacher was up against it. When he was on the witness stand he confessed he had not expected the Lord to answer his prayer. The jury held that it was an act of providence and that the preacher was not responsible for anything the Lord might do.

The term "blind pig," used to describe an illegal bar, is synonymous with "blind tiger," which was first employed in the mid–nineteenth century. Someone wrote the term above an opening in a wall in an arcade, but when patrons paid for a view of the blind pig or tiger, they received a shot of whiskey through the opening instead. The absurdity of viewing "blind" animals was an obvious front for alcohol distribution.

At that time, the only help I was to Doctor was moral support. He took me everywhere he went, and we had our little jokes as we traveled country roads. In the summertime, if a jack rabbit jumped out of a wheat field, Doctor would say, "This is my wheat field and I like to hide in it and nibble the tender leaves and it's nobody's business." As though a rabbit could talk!

One night we were all night at a farmer's house waiting for a baby to arrive. I lay on the foot of a bed and slept. Doctor, of course, stayed up to take care of the woman. The baby was born near morning and we were invited for breakfast. I didn't want to eat, for the people were very dirty and their house was a mess. Finally, I thought that while Doctor ate I would drink some milk fresh from the cow. I had made the remark that it was good milk when I at once heard a noise behind me. I turned and the dogs were lapping out of the pail of fresh milk.

I never heard the last of that until one day we were in the country and it was long past noon and I was getting hungry. I asked the farmer's wife if I could have some milk. She gave it to me in a glass and then she asked Doctor if he would like some. He said, "Yes, if you have a *glass* I'll have some milk." The poor woman ransacked the cupboard for another glass. Finally, she said, "If you will take it in a *cup*, I'll give you some." Doctor had been talking and not noticed the implication that it must be a glass. After that when he remarked, "This is good milk," I responded, "Yes, if you have a glass I'll take some milk."

In the practice of medicine one has to keep a sense of humor. My husband, being Irish, had more than most. He knew an old doctor in another county who was very ignorant in many ways. He took Doctor into his office one day for a visit. In his window he had a row of bottles filled with an amber colored fluid. He called Doctor's attention to the bottles and said, "Do you see them bottles in the window? Well, that's u-r-I-n-e. You'd be surprised whose urIne that is." He pointed to one bottle, mentioned a woman in his town, and said, "She's a rich woman." He seemed taken with the wonder of it.

Before I had gone away to study medicine, and one morning when the Doctor was out in the country making a usual call, a man came to our house wanting Doctor to extract his tooth. He was a tall, angular person from the country. When he found the Doctor gone he wanted me to take it out for him. I told him I knew nothing about extracting teeth, but he kept insisting. Finally, I said I'd try, but he said he'd go downtown first and get a drink of whiskey.

In a little while he came back, pretty well shot. He cried and got down on the floor on his knees to pray. At last he climbed into our office chair and told me to go ahead. I examined him to see for sure which tooth was bothering him and then selected a forceps. I thought to myself, "I'll pull on it as far into the root as I can and squeeze real tight so it won't slip off." I did this and then exerted a strong, steady pull. Out it came. The man was so overjoyed I thought he might embrace me. He said he would never let anyone else pull his teeth. I took out several for him afterwards.

His wife was even more peculiar. He once came to town bragging that she was going to have a baby. She weighed three hundred pounds and I can't imagine how he knew. When he thought the time was up he had a doctor come from another town. The doctor stayed three days and still no baby. Finally, the doctor went home. Over two years later his wife gave birth to a two and one-half pound baby with three hernias.

People always thought this man and his wife were ludicrous when they came to town. He was so tall and lanky and sat on the edge of the seat while his wife, with her great weight, filled the seat and then some. She had rolls of fat down to her knees, a double chin, and a double stomach; she was all rolling fat.

I had transferred to the Woman's Medical College of Kansas City, Missouri, and graduated in 1901. After I returned to Herndon, Doctor went to Chicago to take a refresher course and left me in charge of the practice.

The school Mary attended was located on the north-east corner of 13th Street and Grand Avenue. Mary's application to practice in Kansas indicated that she took three terms of study altogether over three years, from September 13, 1898, to March 20, 1901. According to Walter Rowland's application to practice medicine in Kansas, he completed three terms of medical instruction from September 25, 1893, to March 25, 1895 (the school admitted him to the second year class on the strength of his previous studies).

The very first case I had on my own was the broken arm of a little girl who had fallen down a stairway. The arm broke and dislocated at the elbow, a difficult location because of the liability of a stiff joint. I fixed it up very carefully and obtained a fine result: a good and flexible joint.

The next case was a broken leg. A family sent a nine-year-old Bohemian boy out at four in the morning on a June day to herd cattle. About ten in the morning he grew sleepy and the cattle were doing all right so he lay down to sleep in the deep rut of the road, shaded by grass. It was time to cut the wheat and some men drove along with a team hitched to a header box, but because the rut was deep and the grass long they didn't see him lying there. The little fellow woke up as the horses were passing over him. He tried to get out, but a wheel caught him across the thigh and broke the bone; it also cut his head.

The men called for me and I put him on a flat bed on his back. Then I ran adhesive tape down both sides of the broken leg and under the foot. I ran a bandage through the tape beneath his foot and to this I attached a flat iron for traction. This method was called Buck's extension. When the femur breaks, the muscles pull the broken ends apart and they do not heal. With continuous pull, however, the muscles give way after awhile and the leg straightens out. There is a modification of Buck's extension used in hospitals today, a great improvement over older methods.

I left the boy to lie that way for several days until Doctor came home to help with the case. Doctor worried that it was not all right. Me, I didn't have a doubt in the world because I had followed the instructions given in our book on minor surgery. I didn't think it could go wrong. When the leg healed, it turned out to be just as long as the other. Within a short time no one knew it had ever been broken.

It is notable that medical schools of the time gave singular attention to proper dressings for broken bones. At Missouri's Kansas City Medical College during Walter's matriculation, the school catalog listed a "Physicians' Supply Co. Prize" of surgical instruments awarded "for the best plaster dressing suitable for fracture of leg."

Doctor and I were speaking one day of what people do when confronted with different situations. I don't think anyone correctly anticipates their actions, but one is always saying, "I would or wouldn't do so and so or use such and such treatment." My mind went back to the first summer after I married. One of our neighbors, a Mrs. George, invited me to go with her to look for wild chokecherries. We went in her spring wagon. She took her boy who was about ten years old then, and buckets to hold the cherries if we found any. We wandered around over the divides and down into a draw. Mrs. George got out of the wagon and went to investigate, telling me to hold the horses.

The bushes turned out to be wild plums and were loaded with ripe fruit. She picked a bucket full before she signaled me to come. I had to drive around to the head of the draw before I was able to get there. By then she was picking her second bucket. I also picked a bucket and just as I had finished, a man came over the hill blustering that we were stealing his plums. He was tall, gaunt, and red-headed, with a flushed face. He berated us and said he'd been watching his plums and now here were a couple of women stealing them. Mrs. George began to talk in a placating way, telling him that she was Mrs. I. N. George, and that I was Mrs. Dr. Rowland. She said that we didn't know the plums belonged to anyone. Then she asked what she should do with them. He told her to pour them right out on the ground, which she did.

In the meantime, I hadn't said a word, but I'd been thinking to myself, "There are no fences anywhere and wild plums are not worth anything, only the picking of them is worth anything. I have picked them and I am just not going to give them up." I took my plums and climbed into the spring wagon, set the bucket between my feet, took hold of the lines, and held the buggy whip in my hand. I never said a word. He looked the situation over and said, "You can keep your plums." If anyone had earlier asked me what I'd have done I wouldn't have expected the outcome. Mrs. George bemoaned her fate all the way home because she'd given up her plums. Doctor thought it was humorous and soon found that the man didn't own the land where the plums grew. I never did like to be bullied.

Now that I had graduated in medicine I wanted a baby of my own. After I became pregnant, however, I was so nauseated that nothing would stay in my stomach. We had been married more than four years and people had forgotten to expect us to have any children. All the neighbors worried about my nausea and thought I had eaten something disagreeable. One old lady, a foreigner who lived next door, told me, "Grease your belly, grease your belly." These people who had seemed so queer to me at first had become my friends and I had learned that they were just people like me. Later, when this dear old soul knew my ailment, she reproached me, saying, "Vy did'n you tell me?"

I look back through the years at the long quiet time of my gestation, and I remember hoping it would be a girl. When a woman enters into the delivery of her unborn child, she enters a realm where no one really goes with her. In a way it is like death. We die alone always. The mother gives birth to her child alone. No one else ever really knows what it is like. The father, the doctor, and the nurse may stand around, but they are not exactly a part of it. The doctor understands the mechanics of childbirth, but does not feel it. There is some mysterious attachment between the mother and child which nothing but death ever severs. The father feels the responsibility of caring for both, but he knows nothing of the mystery of mother love.

My brother, who lived twenty miles from Goodland, Kansas, lost his wife in confinement. The placenta was

in front of the baby and the mother bled to death before
the doctor could get there.

Today placenta previa *is routinely handled through
Caesarean section delivery.*

The mother left my brother with three children. My
mother had gone to be with my brother and his wife
and she expected to be back to my house to be with me
too, as we expected our baby in late May. However, on
April 24, just four days after brother Ben's tragedy, I
began to feel slight contractions over my abdomen. My
good neighbor and friend came to stay with me while
the Doctor went to the country to make a professional
call. Later in the evening Doctor and I sat out on the
porch as it was quite warm. He made the remark that he
guessed my contractions would pass, but I informed
him that they were coming at regular intervals.

We went to bed, but Doctor was too anxious about
me to sleep. I urged him to try to sleep on the couch in
the front room, but he kept popping into the bedroom to
see how I felt. About two o'clock in the morning he insisted we send for Mrs. Schwab, but I made him let her
sleep until it was necessary. Poor man, it must have
been hard for him to keep his lonely vigil. I wasn't
lonely, for I was doing a piece of work I had long
looked forward to. At seven o'clock the next morning I
asked for Mrs. Schwab. She had had a good night's
sleep. It was not that I needed her, but I thought Doctor
would feel better able to take care of the rest of it if she
were present.

About noon I asked for some chloroform and Doctor
said, "Now, the time to take chloroform is when the

pains get hard." Then I said very emphatically, "I am having these pains and I know whether they are hard or not. I want some chloroform." I certainly was getting bossy. Doctor made an examination and announced that the baby was coming right along. At half past one o'clock our baby was born and I asked if it was a girl. Doctor was busy taking care of me and did not answer so I repeated, "Is it a girl?" Doctor spoke as if exasperated, "Yes, it's a girl!" I began to cry and Mrs. Schwab said, "Now, Mrs. Rowland, you wanted a girl and it's a girl. What are you crying about?" Doctor said to her, "Let her alone, she is drunk on chloroform. She is all right."

On April 25, 1902, the great ordeal was over. As soon as I heard her cry she was mine against the world, and as long as life should last. I loved my husband and now I loved my baby. It seemed that life had given me everything that one could desire. My heart was full of joy. My cup was running over. Surely God had placed his hand on me to bless me. The twenty-third Psalm came to mind: "The Lord is my shepherd. I shall not want."

In our house every one was so glad about the new baby. My stepdaughter was pleased and my eleven-year-old stepson said her face looked like a peach, all fuzzy and round. Doctor took all care for her, and every time he changed her he said, "Missy, you had no business being a girl." She was born on Friday.

An Unthinkable Murder

How quickly one's whole life can change. Here I was with my baby and my husband, and I was getting along just fine with the two stepchildren who were living with us. The day was sunshiny and calm. I felt at peace with the whole world. Doctor had bought some candy to give my guests when they came to call on me. Every time he went through the room he took out a piece of candy and I made the remark that he would eat it all and there would be none left for my company. He said, "O, I'll get some more."

The Doctor had been worrying about one of the merchants of our town with whom he had been on intimate terms. The man suddenly seemed cold and avoided Doctor, although they had been in the habit of exchanging confidences. His name was George W. Dull. His wife and I had been on neighborly terms since I had lived in Herndon. On Monday morning after our baby was born, Doctor brought up the subject with me again. I asked him how he knew Dull had something on his mind and he said, "Well, he used to have some little confidence for me and it was 'Come again Doc.' Now he never speaks unless he has to." Then I said, "He is your brother Mason, if you go to him and ask him he will tell you. You do not know what big lie someone has told him." I thought it would be better to have no misunderstanding, that if they could talk they would clear things up.

He went downtown to pay for a suit of clothes that he had bought a day or two earlier. He had bought them from the other merchant, Dan Schwab. He soon came back with a pair of suspenders that he said Dan had given him. I asked him if he had talked with Dull yet and he said, "No, not yet." I told him that Mrs. Schwab wanted him to come to her house to see her little boy, and as he went out of my room he remarked, "Bradford, poor little fellow, I'm afraid he is not very strong."

Monday morning my baby had not yet taken the breast. I was thinking of that and about what could have upset the relationship between Doctor and Mr. Dull. I speculated how Mrs. Dull had come to our house three weeks before to invite us to a party at her brother's house. I told her I was in no condition to go to a party. Doctor had asked at the time if Mrs. Dull had shown any resentment because we could not go. I told him she had not seemed to.

At eleven-thirty that morning I saw the druggist run across our back yard and I wondered why he was not in his store. He must have gone to our back door, for shortly Clara, my stepdaughter, came to the bedroom door and said the druggist told her to tell me that Doctor would not be home to dinner. Right away I knew something was odd, for if he were in town he would be home and if he had gone to the country he would have told me. In a few minutes, Mrs. Schwab and John Kirchner, the hardware merchant, entered my bedroom. John stood at the foot of my bed while Mrs. Schwab sat on the edge of my bed. They were both very pale and agitated. Mrs. Schwab took my hand and said, "Now, Mrs. Rowland, I don't want you to be worried but the Doctor has been hurt." I said, "Hurt, how?" She said, "We don't know. He was hurt in Dull's flour room." Then I said, "Did something fall on him?" John Kirchner said, "We don't know what happened but it looks like a blow on the head." I said, "Bring him to the house so I can do something for him. Then he is alive." John said, "Yes." I told them to send to Kansas City for the best surgeon possible. When they did not bring him to the house I wanted to get up and go to him. That, of course, they would not let me do.

It turned out that they didn't want to tell me the truth until they had another doctor there to look after me. They sent for Dr. De May, a friend of Doctor's who lived twenty-five miles east of Danbury, Nebraska. There was only one train a day on the branch road connecting Herndon. The train wouldn't get in before four o'clock. All that time I was worrying about Doctor lying there without anything being done for him. How cruel people can be in their efforts to be kind. If I live a thousand years I shall not live as long as I lived that day.

At four o'clock Dr. De May came and was in the next room with Dan Schwab. Dan came into my bedroom and said, "Now Mrs. Rowland, I want to talk to you." I said, "I don't want to talk to you, I want to talk to Dr. De May. You have been here all day, but he can tell me how badly Doctor is hurt." Then Dan said, "Listen, Mrs. Rowland, the Doctor only lived a minute." Suddenly, the bed went out from under me, then the floor, then the whole world went away, and I was suspended in a vacuum.

My husband had been a very popular man and everyone in town came to see me that day but Dull and his wife. In the afternoon in my distress I sent for them inasmuch as it had all happened in Dull's flour room. Dull said he didn't know how the Doctor had been hurt. Then I asked him what they had talked about and he said, "We talked about the weather and the future prospects for a crop." I said, "Is that all you talked about?" He responded, "Yes." I must have been wondering if Doctor had said anything about what had worried us. I think that he and his wife were the only ones in our town who ate anything that day. They both smelled of onions.

According to Mary, Dull once told Walter, "I tell you things I wouldn't want you to tell anybody else." Adding to the mystery, Walter told Mary that, indeed, he wouldn't even tell her some of the things Dull told him.

I think no certainty, however devastating, is ever so terrible as uncertainty. When you have a certainty, it is finished, but an uncertainty leaves you to worry about what to do.

That evening Fred Robertson, the county attorney, and Dr. De May were sitting by the window at the foot of my bed talking about the tragedy. I overheard Fred say that when he arrived he found the Doctor lying in Dull's flour room with his head near the door and Dull came in and said, "Did he say anything?" Some of the men said, "He never said a word." Dull turned and left the flour room. Suddenly, it came into my mind that Doctor had gone down there to ask him why he wasn't friendly anymore. It was never known what hidden thought or secret suspicion lurked in his mind and caused him to shoot down his only intimate friend in cold blood without even giving him time to understand.

My mother had left my brother in his grief to be with me in my confinement. News didn't travel as it does today. She had gone from Goodland to St. Francis to get on the train that passed through Herndon. At St. Francis she heard some men talking and they were saying that the doctor at Herndon had been murdered. She didn't know the baby had come until she got to Atwood; there someone told her a baby was born a few days earlier. My poor mother, to have my brother and me in such great trouble at once. My father arrived from Indianola at three o'clock in the morning and as he sat by my bed I said to him, "O, Pa, isn't this awful?" He responded so softly that I could hardly hear him, "Yes, it is."

When one of your dear ones is ill you have time to reconcile yourself to the possible death, but when tragedy strikes it is like an avalanche, enormous, overwhelming. You think you cannot live but somehow you do. And life goes on.

I buried Doctor by his first wife at Indianola, Nebraska. People were good, especially the Masons. The Masons did many services for me that I didn't at the time know about, but for which I shall always be grateful.

The sheriff arrested Dull, but he was soon out on bond to await his trial which was set for November at Atwood, our county seat. Fred Robertson, the county attorney, was a young man and I thought I should have an experienced lawyer help him at the trial. Tully Scott, a lawyer at Cripple Creek, Colorado, had the reputation of being first-class and I engaged him to help with the prosecution.

I began to practice when my baby was a month old. If I had been wise, I never would have tried to practice while I nursed her. I was practically on the gallop all the time. I would hurry to take care of a patient and then hurry home to nurse the baby. I kept a girl to do the housework and Doctor's mother came and stayed with me for two years to help take care of the baby. I am forever grateful to that gentle creature who was such a comfort to me. Her husband, a Civil War veteran, would come over from their home and stay a day or two at a time. He always entertained her at such times narrating Gettysburg battles. Sometimes, when my mother was there at the same time, listening to some of his stories, she would be insulted and say, "Is his wife silly enough to believe all those wild tales?" I would pacify Mother and tell her it didn't matter if they were true or not. They entertained each other that way and it was just as good as the conversations of many other people.

Before I had practiced two months, I was called to attend a woman who was said to be dying. It was a few miles out in the country. The seventeen-year-old Hungarian girl was eight months pregnant and in convulsions. Her family couldn't speak English, but her husband got a neighbor to translate for us. I gave her one-half grain of morphine knowing that one-fourth grain was a good dose. It controlled the convulsions for the time being. I sent for the help of a young doctor who had come to our town after my husband's death. This doctor was a morphine addict, but there was no other doctor near enough to be of any help. When he arrived I wanted to take the baby, but he disagreed and said, "She will not have any more convulsions." I knew the instructions in such a case were to empty the uterus.

I had arrived there about three o'clock in the afternoon, and after the big shot of morphine she went to sleep and slept until seven. When the convulsions started again the other doctor was willing to have me dilate the uterus and take the baby. On examination I found the baby with a shoulder presenting although labor had not started. When the other doctor examined her he washed his hands, but used no antiseptic. He looked so dirty I hated to have him do anything. In those days we had to work in homes though now doctors have hospitals, sanitary conditions, and plenty of nurses to help. Today the baby would be taken by Caesarean section, relieving the stress on the kidneys. We used chloroform or ether. As ether is explosive in the presence of a blaze, we used chloroform at night. Chloroform is far more dangerous than modern anesthetics.

We placed the woman across the bed and the other doctor gave the chloroform while I began to dilate the uterus. It sounds easy, but the uterus has the strongest muscle in the body and it contracted on my hand like a vise. It was some time before I was able to bring down the baby's foot. When I had succeeded in bringing down both feet and legs, my hand and arm were so paralyzed that I let the other doctor finish delivering the baby. I went to her head to give the chloroform and he began to pull on the baby's feet. After awhile he said, "I can't get the head out." Then I instructed him to let the baby's legs straddle his arm and to slip his finger into the baby's mouth. After doing this the baby flexed its chin onto its chest and slipped right out. It was a living child.

The mother hovered between life and death, but we finally got her kidneys acting and so far as I know they both might be alive today. I might add a few words about the other doctor. He died in the jail at Atwood from an overdose of morphine. They said he went crazy and was so obstreperous that they couldn't handle him except in jail. We had no law against the illicit use of narcotics then. I have often wondered how much instruction in medicine he had really had. I thought that my patient that day might die from infection because the doctor was so dirty.

Later that summer I was called to care for a severely hemorrhaging woman. She was pregnant six months and I determined that the placenta was located over the cervix and had become partially detached. To keep her from bleeding to death, as Doctor's patient had, I packed her with sterile gauze immediately. Then I waited some six hours for the uterus to contract and expel the contents. It was an anxious time for me as I didn't feel too sure that the bleeding had stopped. The husband was eager to have a living baby and he expected me to save the mother and the baby.

When I removed the gauze everything was ready to come away, but the baby was dead. The father blamed me for killing his only child. As I look back, with more experience I might have explained the situation better. But then, perhaps he thought he needed a good excuse for not paying his bill. He never did, nor could he later find any good in me. Oh, well! Doctors have to take those things. I was learning fast. Doctors are often the scapegoats when something goes wrong.

Later in the month I went into the shop of August Kleint, the butcher, to get some meat when I noticed that his helper had an eruption on his face. I said to him, "Willie, what is the matter with you?" He said, "The other doctor said I had an eruption that was going around." The other doctor was the drug addict. Then I said, "Willie, lean over here and let me feel that eruption." I remembered the descriptions of the different contagious diseases. Smallpox is first a temperature and an eruption of macules, then the temperature goes down and the macules become papules that feel like shot under the skin. That was the way Willie's forehead felt.

August was in the country so I left word for him to come to my office as soon as possible. He came in a short while later and I told him that Willie had smallpox and for him to take him to the county pesthouse or his shop would be quarantined at once. Willie stayed in the back room of the butcher shop until they could get the pesthouse in order with supplies.

The man whose baby had died when I cared for his wife went to the window, looked at Willie, and said, "He hasn't any more smallpox than I have." It was hard for him to believe I knew anything.

I visited Willie from time to time and we had the county doctor down from Atwood who verified my diagnosis. In a few days Willie looked as though he had pumpkin seeds sticking out all over him. When he came back to town with his face all pockmarked no one was willing even then to say it had been smallpox. I believe I saved that community from an epidemic of the disease, for scarcely anyone had been vaccinated. I somehow did not resent that it was hard for people to believe in a woman doctor. It was so new.

One day on my way to the bank, as I was passing Dull's store, he came out and said, "How do you do, Mrs. Rowland?" There came such a feeling over me that I knew if I had had anything to do with it, I would have killed him on the spot. I whirled and said, "Don't you ever speak to me again, you murderer, you!"

In the fall I went to Atwood to be at the trial. I stayed with the county attorney's mother. They had a hard time getting a jury because almost everyone had an opinion about the case. One subpoenaed German said, when asked if he had an opinion on the case, "No, but I tink he's guilty."

The Trial Document

The following is reprinted from the Supreme Court of Kansas case record number 13,396: "The State of Kansas v. George W. Dull" (Vol. 67, July Term, 1903). While the document's language is archaic, it is a period piece and the best available summary of the murder and trial. Dull was convicted of second degree murder in Rawlins District Court and appealed to the Supreme Court of Kansas. The Supreme Court upheld the conviction. Dull was later pardoned by a governor of Kansas. This summary describes the murder as "Singular, mysterious, and inscrutable . . ."

Homicide—Proof of Motive Not Indispensable. In contemplation of law every sane man is presumed to intend the natural and reasonable consequences of his own act. Hence, on the trial of one charged with murder, if it be proved beyond a reasonable doubt to the satisfaction of the jury that defendant killed the deceased, proof of the motive which actuated the defendant thereto, while always proper, is not indispensable.

—Malice Inferred from Deadly Weapon. When on the trial of one charged with murder the accused denies all knowledge of or participation in the act of killing, it is proper for the court to instruct the jury that if it be found from the evidence beyond a reasonable doubt that defendant killed the deceased with a deadly weapon, malice in law may be inferred from the fact that defendant used a deadly weapon.

Appeal from Rawlins District Court; John R. Hamilton, judge. Opinion filed November 7, 1903. Affirmed.

C. C. Coleman, attorney-general, J. H. Briney, Fred Robertson, and Tully Scott, for The State.

John E. Hessin, for appellant.

About eleven o'clock on the morning of April 18, 1902, in the little town of Herndon, Rawlins County, Doctor Rowland was twice shot with a 38-caliber revolver, one bullet passing through his head and the other through his heart, killing him almost instantly. The killing was done in a room called the flour-room, attached to and forming a part of the general merchandise store building of the defendant. The defendant and deceased had resided in this town for many years. Both were married. They and their families, in so far as shown by the evidence, had lived in intimate and friendly relations. On the morning of the tragedy Doctor Rowland appeared at the store, spoke to the defendant saying, "Good morning, George, where is Jesse [a clerk]? I want to speak to you." At the time defendant was sitting upon a lounge or settee in the storeroom near the front door, wearing neither coat nor vest. The two walked a few feet into the flour-room and stood near the front door leading from the street into that room. People passing observed them so standing and talking in an apparently friendly but interested manner. The evidence further shows that within a few seconds after being last observed so standing and talking, two shots were fired. The deceased was found lying where he had stood talking. There were powder marks upon his face, hand, and collar, hence it is evident the shots were fired at close range. It also appears that the shots were fired from the direction in which the defendant was last seen standing, if deceased remained standing in the same position he had occupied. When first seen after the shooting the defendant was sitting at his desk in the rear of the store at work upon his accounts, seemingly unperturbed. When by his clerk apprised of the killing he went at once to the deceased, prepared a pillow for his head, and in other ways assisted in ministering to his wants. While the testimony shows there was conversation between defendant and deceased on the morning of the tragedy in relation to some chattel mortgage property, yet the record tends to show the visit made by deceased to the defendant was made with the knowledge of the wife of deceased, who, after the tragedy, sent for defendant to come to her bedside, where she lay sick and prostrated, and with great solicitation inquired whether the weather and the crop prospects were all they had talked about just prior to the tragedy, to which defendant responded "yes."

*April 18 is a typo in the court document. The correct
date is April 28.*

Upon the firing of the shots the flour-room was filled
with smoke. One witness, passing, claims to have seen
the legs of someone retreating through a ware-room in
the rear of the flour-room just after the shooting occurred. There was a passageway back through this
ware-room by which the defendant could have gone after the shooting to his desk where seen just after the
tragedy. A door in the rear of this ware-room which fastened from the inside was found unfastened and slightly
ajar after the killing. The shots were fired from a
38-caliber weapon. Defendant owned a 38-caliber revolver. He was in the habit of carrying it to and from
his store in the morning and evening, as he carried cash
in some amounts from the store to his home. This revolver was afterwards secured from the defendant, and
when secured all the chambers were found loaded, two
of which bore evidence of having been recently fired.
This condition of the weapon was accounted for by evidence of the defendant and his wife that he had fired
two shots at rats at his home.

No person other than defendant, deceased, and the
clerk in the store was seen around the store near the
time of the tragedy. No one was seen leaving the building. It was not shown that deceased had any enemy who
had ever threatened his life or would be inclined to
compass his death.

Defendant was arrested, charged with the crime of
murder in the first degree; tried, and convicted of murder in the second degree, and appeals to this court.

The principal points in the evidence are presented in

the briefs of counsel. This evidence, on the one hand, discloses almost an entire want of motive on the part of the defendant to design or accomplish the death of deceased. On the other hand, there is in the evidence an entire absence of any plausible theory by which the deceased could have come to his death save at the hands of defendant. A case more barren of testimony upon the two features mentioned can scarcely be conceived, and fortunately for those whose duty it is to assist in the enforcement of the law, seldom occurs.

The principal objection urged against the judgment of conviction is an utter want of evidence in its support. The evidence is circumstantial, the cause of the homicide shrouded in mystery. No motive on the part of the defendant to commit the deed is shown, yet, upon all the facts and circumstances in the case that go to make up the evidence found in the record, under the law as given by the court, the jury, with the witnesses for and against the accused face to face, assumed the responsibility of declaring the guilt of the accused. This declaration of guilt has been upheld by the trial court, better able to judge of the manner, demeanor, and credibility of the witnesses than is this court. Hence, it is now too late again to draw into controversy the question of the guilt or innocence of the accused, unless it may be said that there is an entire absence of testimony upon some essential element of the crime vital to a conviction, or the trial court has, as shown by the record, misjudged the law to the prejudice of the accused.

No defense is interposed save that the deed was not done by the defendant. When the evidence found in the record is fully considered in all its bearings; when it is remembered that immediately prior to the tragedy deceased and defendant were seen together, standing in such relative positions that had the shots been fired by the defendant they would probably have struck the deceased where the wounds resulting in death were made; that the balls which caused the death were fired from a weapon of the same caliber as that found in the possession of the accused thereafter, two chambers of which weapon had been recently discharged; the utter improbability, not to say impossibility, of the wounds having been inflicted either by the hand of the deceased or that of a third person; the fact that the accused admits having heard the shots fired in such close proximity to him without concern or investigation, when the firing did attract the immediate attention of others in the vicinity; the further fact that the interview between deceased and defendant was sought by deceased and intended to be of a private nature; the route taken by the accused from the place of his interview with deceased to the place where he was first seen after the tragedy was committed; the improbability of the testimony of accused that when the interview closed he left deceased standing where he was immediately thereafter found dying, and that he had no knowledge of the commission of the tragedy—when these facts are considered with all the other facts and circumstances in the case, as shown by the record, the mind is of necessity almost irresistibly compelled to the conclusion that defendant must have committed the deed, although what motive, if any, actuated him thereto lies hidden in his breast, is not known, and may never be discovered until the last great day.

Conceding then, as we must, sufficient evidence found in the record to support the verdict of guilt, did the trial court err in the matter of law to the prejudice of the defendant? Upon the question of motive the charge to the jury reads:

"The presence or absence of a motive for the alleged commission of an alleged crime is always an important ingredient for the consideration of the jury in determining the guilt or the innocence of the person charged, yet when the accused is shown beyond a reasonable doubt, even if only by circumstantial evidence, to be the perpetrator of the alleged crime, it is not necessary that there be proof of motive, there is no occasion for explaining the reason of his acts. Every man of sane mind is presumed to intend the reasonable and natural consequences of his own acts."

We think this instruction correctly states the law.

Complaint is made of the manner of endorsing names on the information and its authentication by the prosecuting attorney. In this there was no error.

The only question of merit arising upon the law of the case is found in the charge of the court to the jury. Instruction 8 reads:

"When the killing is done with a deadly weapon or a weapon calculated to produce death, malice may be legitimately inferred in the absence of proof that the act was done in necessary self-defense or upon sufficient provocation or cause, and the presumption in such case will be that the act was voluntarily committed with malice aforethought."

Was the giving of this instruction error? Mr. Bishop, in his work on criminal law, Vol. 2, Sec. 680, says:

"As a general doctrine, subject, we shall see, to some qualifications, the malice of murder is conclusively inferred from the unlawful use of a deadly weapon, resulting in death."

In the case of Commonwealth v. York, 9 Metc. 93, 94, 43 Am. Dec. 373, it was held:

"The rule of law is, when the fact of killing is proved to have been committed by the accused, and nothing further is shown, the presumption of law is that it is malicious, and an act of murder. It follows, therefore, that in such cases the proof of matter of excuse or extenuation lies on the accused; and this may appear, either from evidence adduced by the prosecution, or evidence offered by the defendant."

In the case of State v. Earnest, 56 Kan. 31, 42 Pac. 359, this court held:

"On the trial of a person charged with murder, the jury ought not to be instructed that the killing with a deadly weapon being admitted, the presumption therefore is that such killing was with malice, and that this presumption stands until it is rebutted by evidence. It would be better to instruct them that malice may be inferred from the fact of killing with a deadly weapon, and that they should consider this circumstance in connection with all the other evidence in the case for the purpose of determining whether the act was malicious or not."

From the whole charge the jury are advised if the one disputed fact, the act of killing, be first found against the accused beyond a reasonable doubt, the proof of motive for the commission of the deed may be dispensed with, and the essential ingredient in the crime of murder, malice, may be inferred from the use of a deadly weapon as the instrument employed to accomplish the deed. This we think proper, and the claim of error is disallowed.

It is further urged that, as there were no mitigating or

extenuating circumstances shown or attempted to be shown in the killing, the verdict of murder in the second degree found no support in the testimony, and the jury should have been instructed to convict the defendant of murder in the first degree, or acquit, as they might find the fact of killing for or against the accused. There is, however, slight evidence found in the record which gives warrant to a charge of murder in the second degree and sustains the judgment. Aside from this, however, the evidence is circumstantial, and the jury may have failed to find from all the facts and circumstances in the case the deliberation and premeditation essential to uphold a verdict in the higher degree. In the case of The State v. Moore, ante, page 620, 73 Pac. 905, this court held:

"If, upon the trial of a defendant informed against for murder in the first degree, circumstantial evidence relied on for conviction be susceptible of interpretation in such manner as to exclude deliberation and premeditation, an instruction upon the law of murder in the second degree should be given."

Singular, mysterious, and inscrutable as was the killing of the deceased by the defendant, as found by the jury in this case, yet, the jury upon sufficient evidence having found the act of killing to have been done by the defendant, and no justification therefore having been shown, and no error of law appearing in the record, the conviction must stand.

All the Justices concurring.

Telling All

Typically Victorian, Mary presumed that including in her memoirs the court summary, a brief description of events and feelings, and a rudimentary sentence saying that George Dull was later pardoned for the murder of Walter Rowland would answer readers' questions. Of course, the analytical observer has much deeper curiosity.

Mary sent the Rawlins County attorney and Tully Scott to Topeka to contest the appeal to the Supreme Court of Kansas. After the Supreme Court decided against the defendant, Dull was sentenced to twenty years in the penitentiary. Mary learned that the Masons expelled him and his insurance was canceled. A few years after she left Herndon, the block that included Dull's store burned to the ground. Mary later said she was thankful she had not lived in Herndon at the time.

Dull served several years until March 1, 1907, when the governor of Kansas pardoned him. The Dull family's efforts to obtain the pardon began in the administration of W. J. Bailey, governor of Kansas from 1903 to 1905. Dull did not receive a pardon from Governor Bailey. The second effort was successful during the administration of Governor E. W. Hoch, who served from 1905 to 1909. Both campaigns included citizen petitions, letters from suppliers to Dull's store, validation of good behavior from the prison warden, legal arguments that circumstantial evidence is not enough to convict a man of murder, a petition showing the names of two jurors who agreed that a pardon should be given to Dull, and one letter from Dull's attorney to Governor Bailey implying private knowledge bearing on the case that would only be conveyed to the governor. This effort incensed Mary who, with other citizens, friends, relatives, and jurors, wrote to both governors opposing a pardon.

The effort to get the two jurors to sign the petition on behalf of Dull must have been aggressive as they both wrote notes later to Governor Hoch saying they had been misinformed or confused about the petition they had signed. Quoting from juror Paulson's note: "The petition i singed in the Dul cas it was repisented to me that one of the judges of the Sup Cort says the evidence was not suficent for conviction is why i signed petiton but i stil beleive him guilty." [sic] Said juror Murphy: "I signed (Petition) With the Under-Standing that all the Jurors Would Sign it—I didn't Want to be in opposition to all of the rest. I understood the Judge was to Sign it. I am Still of the impression that g.W. Dull is guilty." [sic]

After the trial, Mary's loneliness and desire for a companion's support led her into a relationship with August Kleint, the Herndon butcher. Two years later she married August and he left the meat-cutting business to enter real estate. Mary became convinced that she had made a mistake and married too quickly on *the rebound. There is a scotched sentence still readable in her original typewritten manuscript which says, "That very thing [a desire for support] caused me to make the greatest mistake of my life." Mary and August were ultimately incompatible and the marriage ended effectively when August left Topeka for Idaho in June of 1908. A divorce was granted to Mary in 1909 on grounds of incompatibility.*

In Idaho, August entered into a joint venture with Mary's brother-in-law Perry Ginther, her sister Nellie's husband. In the last years of her life, Mary said that she had remained friendly with August in Idaho to help him get a new start. Other sources—friends and relatives in the Idaho community—suggest that ambivalence about the relationship lingered for several years. In any case, August was in the picture from 1904 to 1909.

August and Perry ran a small lumber mill on Poison Creek near the mouth of the Gold Fork River. The mill ran into financial difficulty and Perry and Nellie moved on to Oregon. August, however, stayed in the Gold Fork area and started another mill that fared much better. After he had made some money he bought a ranch at the foot of West Mountain. Unable to make payments in full, however, he too sold out and moved on to Oregon.

After the separation, Mary said that Perry, who taught Sunday school, would not speak to her and referred to her as "that divorcee." While this appears to have miffed Mary, she still respected her brother-in-law Perry. Overall, he had a reputation as a hard worker, teacher, and builder. A strict father, he and Nellie raised children that were happy and outgoing.

*They encouraged their children to obtain educations
and enjoy music. Perry even played a horn in the
town band in Lebanon, Oregon. When Perry suffered
a stroke in the early 1950s, Dr. Mary Rowland attended him at his request.*

*August's children remember him as a good father
and a quiet and respected man who spoke some broken German well into his later years. August's second
wife, who was also from Kansas, told their children
that his marriage to Mary was annulled after August
learned that Mary only wanted him to raise her
daughter Nellie while she practiced medicine. It is
evident from Mary's daughter Nellie's stories about
August that he took care of her occasionally when
she was a little girl. It is also evident that Mary
was a busy professional who liked her work and
sought outside care for her daughter when she could
obtain it.*

*August's wife also told their children about gossip
in Kansas that followed Dull's imprisonment: that
Walter had died because he was "fooling around"
with George Dull's wife. Nothing about these suggested extramarital interests, however, was introduced or alluded to at the murder trial. Dull's
defense, both during and after the trial, was generally that circumstantial evidence should not be
enough to convict him or make his murder sentence
hold. Dull never admitted to having fired a malicious
shot, out of passion or any other reason.*

*The correspondence written to the governor of
Kansas from Dull's attorney referencing private infor-
mation bearing on the case included a letter from
Mrs. Dull to her brother. Dull's attorney suggested*

that this letter provided discrete evidence that was to help the governor make up his mind regarding a pardon for Dull. The attorney asked that the governor not include the confidential letter in the Dull case records; therefore the letter is lost to history.

If the letter implied that Walter had made untoward advances to Mrs. Dull and that she had told her husband about them or that she confessed to having had an affair with Walter, it still does not verify it. After all, Walter's death precluded any rebuttal on his part and the nature of such an involvement implies the unlikelihood that anyone else in the community knew anything about it. During the long trial period, which included an appeal to the Kansas Supreme Court, there is no information in the public record indicating that the idea was circulated or that there was any private party who knew about it. Only after George Dull's imprisonment did the idea appear to surface.

It could as easily be argued that Mrs. Dull tried to interest Walter and was rebuffed, then wanted him punished. Or it could have been a ruse by the attorney or the Dull family after the fact to aid the case for a pardon. Perhaps Mrs. Dull designed the story to encourage her husband to get even with the Rowlands for a social slight such as not attending her brother's party. Perhaps she unleashed something that got out of control. Then again, perhaps Dull was just a very jealous man.

If it were true, did Dull never reveal it because it was too humiliating? And why would Walter have so boldly approached Dull or mentioned his concerns to his wife if he worried that someone had discovered his philandering?

Another circumstance that bears noting is that Walter had a longstanding dislike for the hotel proprietor in Herndon. Mary mentions in her memoirs that he had at one time slandered Walter. Who knows what mischief this man may have stirred up against Walter, through George Dull or otherwise?

There also remain questions concerning the governors: why would a governor be willing to give weight to a letter that implied facts never considered in court? Did the governor provide the pardon based solely or partly on suggestions presented by the letter, even when such suggestions may have only hinted at a motive for murder? The mysterious letter was first made available to Governor Bailey, yet he did not act on behalf of the Dulls. Why did Governor Hoch?

It is possible that favors were in order or that Governor Hoch acted as he did out of expediency. Afterwards, he was very solicitous of Dull to see that he had done well by his decision. And Dull's responses to the governor's inquiries appear supplicating and simple. Dull's lawyer presented his case to the governors in a persistently friendly manner designed to nurture them into his viewpoint, in one letter saying, "I feel interested more than the mere lawyer and only hope you may see the matter as I do."

Some observers will also speculate on these other aspects: Mary was about to give birth and was probably disinclined to sexual activity; Walter traveled freely, in one instance immediately upon Mary's return from a long absence; and Walter visited his young female students, Mary and her roommate May, *without a chaperone, perhaps not wholly in keeping with the social mores of that day.*

It is still not entirely understood why Mary felt such a strong alienation from August after their marriage. While she was sometimes reluctant to acknowledge the parity of English and non-English-speaking citizens, it would be inaccurate to describe her as xenophobic. August was, in fact, bilingual, with a heavy German accent. Mary said within the family that she and August had different interests, which may have been a way of saying that she did not feel August supported her medical career.

It is also conceivable that August alienated Mary with a comment insinuating Walter's infidelity, as there was gossip to this effect during Dull's pursuit of a pardon. At the same time, the Kansas State Historical Society's records include loyal and earnest letters that August, on behalf of his wife Mary, wrote to both governors of Kansas opposing the pardon of George Dull.

Mary's daughter Nellie spoke of August fondly, saying that he was always kind to her. From Mary's account one cannot tell how long the two lived together. In her later years, Nellie could not remember when she last lived with August. They probably lived together for awhile in Topeka before the divorce.

Within several years following the trial, Mary's stepchildren went to live with Walter's family. Mary's parents divorced, though the circumstances of the divorce remain unknown. Her mother, Ellen Crockford Canaga, thereafter married Captain Charles Henry (C. H.) Barrett, a Civil War veteran who fought at Gettysburg.

Restless Years

In this chapter Mary discusses medical training for women in her day and begins to describe her singular practice as a woman doctor. She soon leaves Herndon to obtain another medical degree in Omaha. Upon graduating, she takes a vacation trip to Idaho and Oregon. The text flow is somewhat abrupt as case descriptions are worked in with introspection, travel notes, and philosophy.

I realized how much support my husband had given me in everything I did. Now I had to lean on myself, though I wanted to lean on someone.

It is difficult for me to describe the next few years of my life even after all the intervening years. I had to adjust my life to something I had never contemplated. I had to think of the future and what I was going to do for my child, Nellie. She had cried the first four months, but as time went on she developed into a plump creature. She was small-boned like her father, with brown eyes and light hair. She was and is the greatest joy of my life. All my thoughts and plans had her in mind.

Walter smoked tobacco until Mary became pregnant, then stopped and put on a few extra pounds. Overall, he was thin. Mary told Nellie when Nellie was eight or nine, "I hope you won't have your father's tern legs."

I was always careful to select the right kind of girl to take care of my house because I also had to leave Nellie with her. One couple wanted to adopt her, saying that I could not practice medicine and raise her, but I felt that she was my responsibility and I could not turn her over to someone else for care. I know my thoughts dwelled too much on the tragedy that had come into my life, but as time went on the memories softened and often as I was driving along the highways making calls I remembered an amusing incident that had occurred when Doctor was with me.

Once when Doctor and I were going up a little hill south of town, driving Prince and Lady, something scared the horses and they started to run. Doctor dropped the lines and jumped out of the buggy and ran to their head to stop them. I picked up the lines and laughed and Doctor said, "Madam, this is no laughing matter!" I said, "Well, why didn't you pull on the lines? That is what the lines are for, to control your team."

Another time he was telling me about a girl and her mother who came to have the girl examined. The mother worried while the girl strenuously denied having had anything to do with a man. On examination, Doctor told her she was going to have a baby and the girl said, "No Sir, No Sir, we only tried it once and then just for a moment."

It was never necessary to ask Doctor for money. Occasionally he looked in my purse to see how much was there and then his little joke was, "Now what did you do with that fifty cents I gave you three weeks ago?" as he put more money in.

After I graduated from medical school and was making money of my own, he was letting me pay the bills until one day I said, "Just how much do you expect me to pay?" He gave me a knowing look and said, "Why, I expect you to pay all I can get you to pay." He was always making a list of what he owned and he always listed me at fifteen cents.

Doctors have changed their methods and their medicines greatly since 1900. Formerly, the family doctor was a devoted slave to his work. He went when called, day or night, rain or shine, and never thought to ask if patients could pay their bills. Always faithful to his work, the patient's problems were his problems. He knew all the ailments and quirks of each of his flock. He took his medicine bags on calls and after examining the patient sat down, mixed medicines, put them into powders, and gave directions.

Doctors used to take whatever their patients had to offer in compensation, but it often happened that in a doctor's declining years it was difficult to make ends meet. It was many years before doctors began to be more diligent about collections, as well as to do good by their patients.

In the medical schools students were instructed, when treating a patient, to look after all "the emunctories," meaning the bowels, kidneys, and the skin. If there was no obstruction of the bowels a good strong dose of calomel followed by Epsom salts cured many ailments. I do not mean to give the impression that calomel and Epsom salts were the only medicines used, but it was common practice to "clean out the emunctories."

In speaking of doctors I use the masculine gender. There were at the time when I studied medicine few women doctors. With the great incubation of ideas among men, however, women were incubating a few of their own. Women had delivered babies for ages without any scientific knowledge, but "She" began to want to know the *why* and the *how*. Most of the medical colleges would not admit women. The argument against women studying medicine was much like the argument against women being allowed to vote. They said medicine was indecent for women to know, and that the polls were not a fit place for them to be. The change in the public's attitude toward women represents one of the greatest changes that has ever taken place.

The 1895 preamble of the first annual announcement of the medical school Mary attended, Woman's Medical College of Kansas City, Missouri, stated: "Experience has demonstrated that co-education in medicine has not met with general approval and support; but medical colleges designed exclusively for women are greatly appreciated and are demanded by the better classes. . . . It has been the aim of the promoters of this College to make it first-class in all respects and worthy the exalted position medicine should occupy in every community. Those who object to women being allowed the same educational privileges as men are not in the van; the spirit of the present age is liberality, and the old barriers are being fast torn down, and the doors of all scientific depart-

*ments, all avenues of learning, all vocations of life,
regardless of sex or creed, are being thrown open.
Mentally and morally, it is conceded by all, that
woman is man's equal, and the time has gone by
when physical force with the civilized classes shall
dominate."*

The last fifty years have caused a vast change in men's
attitudes toward women because women have distinguished themselves in so many ways. I have found
more prejudice among the laity than in my profession,
though one doctor once said to me that the reason some
women would rather go to a man doctor is that they
"like to be manhandled," whatever that means.

We had a midwife in our community, and as she often got into trouble with her cases she frequently called
for me. I could have stopped her from practicing, but I
thought she needed the money. One of her patients had
been in labor three days and still there was no baby.
The midwife said she couldn't tell how the baby was
presenting. On examination, I discovered that it was
normal, but that the sac holding the baby had not ruptured. The parts below were well-dilated. I separated the
blades of my scissors and inserted one blade alongside
my finger. When I came to the membrane, I ran the
blade through the sac and out came more than a gallon
of fluid which saturated the bed and the floor beneath it.
In thirty minutes the baby was born. Those people sang
my praises from then on.

Fifteen miles southeast of Herndon I took care of a
man who had received a severe head injury. He was
Swedish and owned a large ranch with some sixty head
of cattle and other stock. His son worked for him and

lived in the same house. His son had a wife and several children, but the older man's wife had died.

The father had a habit of telling obscene stories while seated at the breakfast table. The son had warned him several times to desist, but the old fellow must have had a mean streak for he persisted. One morning the son became so exasperated that he picked the old man up and threw him out the door. The wagon was standing in front of the house and his head struck the wheel and knocked him unconscious, tearing a great wound in his scalp. The son was so angry that he offered no aid. The old fellow lay there until four o'clock in the afternoon when he finally dragged himself to a neighbor who sent for me.

When I arrived he began to quibble about who should pay for my services. He wanted the county to pay. I told him he lived in the wrong county and, if the county was going to pay the doctor bill, he would have to get the county doctor from his own county. The old fellow had bled so much that he could hardly sit in a chair. He finally decided that if I would take a cow in payment he would have me take care of him.

His scalp lay open from just above the eye, back over the ear, and down the back of his head nearly to the hairline. I stood behind him and as I started to clean out the wound I opened the temporal artery which began to spurt blood. It frightened me so much that I almost fainted. I put my finger on the artery just in front of the ear and bore down. For a minute I couldn't see a thing, but I stood there until I felt better, then finished cleaning the wound and put in the stitches. Those people never knew how near their doctor came to toppling over onto the floor.

When I got him taken care of, I told him that I wanted a good cow for it. His wound healed and later in the spring he came to me leading a fine cow. He said he was very grateful.

I was the first doctor in our county in Kansas to use newly introduced antitoxin. I had received almost all the patronage of the Swedish settlement south of Herndon where two little children had developed diphtheria. They made a quick recovery with shots of antitoxin. A year later two other Swedish girls across the road had diphtheria and the parents sent for me. My own baby was just then recovering from *cholera infantum*.

When I arrived to make an examination of the children, I found them suffering. I was afraid to take care of them because of the intimate care I was giving to my baby, therefore I told them that I would send the county doctor with antitoxin. The county doctor put off going for two days and, when he finally went, forgot to take the antitoxin. It was another day before the children received it and they both died.

The distracted mother blamed me for their deaths. She became unbalanced and came to my house where she raved and upbraided me for not taking care of her little girls. She said that I had saved the children of her neighbor, but had refused to treat hers. Now they were dead. Suddenly, she drew out a butcher knife and said she was going to kill me, but her husband and another man finally subdued her. She was sent to the state hospital where she eventually recovered.

There was a small parochial school near the Catholic Church. Three sisters taught the school and whenever they were ill I cared for them. They were sweet women and devoted to their work. I was also often in contact with the local priest. Generally, when someone was sick, the priest beat me to the patient and did a ceremony over them. One night I saw a man who was suffering with quinsy (peritonsillar abscess). He was sitting in a chair with a quilt wrapped around him and had been there for three days without any sleep. I was just ready to lance his throat when Father Wenzel arrived. He came hurrying in and said, "Is there any immediate danger?" I said, "No, please hold the lamp so that I can see where to put in the lance." He helped and the poor creature was so relieved after the lancing that he went right off to sleep as soon as it drained.

I never had any trouble with the priest. It has always been my attitude that a man has a right to his beliefs and if he gets comfort from them, and is willing for me to have mine, why should I interfere with him? Life and death are great mysteries. Man gropes for a solution always, but who really knows?

The climatic conditions made it extremely difficult at times to enjoy driving. The wind often blew up so much dust during calls to the country that upon returning home it was impossible to tell the color of my hair. My eyes were also full of dust. One call I made, I remember very well. It was winter, had been snowing all day, and the wind was drifting the snow into great mounds covering the roads. I had to go some fifteen miles from Herndon to see a man ill with typhoid fever. The sun was going down as I arrived at his home, which meant a night drive back to Herndon.

All our roads had deep ruts and in the dark and drifted snow I was unable to see them. I was in terror all the way home for fear that the horses would get two wheels into a rut and two upon the bank, thus tipping the buggy over. It was late when I at last made my way to the barn. I was so exhausted that to lie down and die would have been a relief. I got the harness off, fed the team, and went into the house to feed my baby. Sometimes after tiring calls, when I began to undress and found that my clothes would not come off easily, I jerked at them and tore them off.

Once, caught out in a violent storm, my horses turned around in the road and wouldn't travel a step. The wind and rain together with the thunder and lightning made it terrifying. Suddenly lightning struck the fence not fifty feet from the place where I sat in the buggy. My horses were cowering and wanted to run, but I held them until the storm abated.

In Kansas and Nebraska one must always fight the elements. It always seemed too hot or too cold or too dry or too dusty. I have always thought that the reason the Sioux Indians were the strongest of all the Indian tribes was that they had to fight the midwestern weather.

I found it easier to take care of one horse than bother with two, so I sold the little mare. One weekend I drove over to spend a little time with my mother who lived in McCook, some twenty miles north of Herndon. Since she lived in the outskirts of town, I put old Prince out on a lariat rope for the night. The next morning, Captain Barrett, my stepfather, came to my room and said, "Mary, I've got more bad news for you. Prince has broken his leg." It had rained in the night and a colt had come along to play. We could see where Prince had gone round and round at the end of his lariat playing with the colt. He somehow wrapped the rope around his leg, slipped, fell, and broke it. I wanted to have it set, but Mother and the Captain told me it would be impractical. I had the town marshal come and shoot my beautiful horse. The marshal, who had known my husband, told someone that he had never hated to do anything so badly as shoot Dr. Rowland's horse.

I could have stayed in Herndon all my life, but I was full of big dreams and had never intended to stay in so small a place. Doctor's passing spoiled the town for me. Discontent, ambition, and curiosity were inducements to continue my growth.

It was my intention to attend Creighton University School of Medicine [John A. Creighton Medicine College] because I needed more training. So much thought had been given to grief and my little girl's future; now it was necessary to go back to school.

The medical college in Topeka, Kansas, where I took my first two years of study, had an exceptional group of men who treated the three women, including myself, as companions. We all enjoyed the lectures, the dissecting, and everything about the school. Two of the men who used to go over the lessons with me became missionaries to China after they graduated. After two years there, I finished school in Kansas City, Missouri, where there were excellent clinics that treated women.

When I went to Creighton Medical at Omaha, however, I noticed a great difference in the attitude of the men. Creighton is a Catholic school and I thought the difference was due to the church's attitude toward women. Some of the students got me off to one side and told me they didn't think the other woman student should be there because she wasn't married, then they got her off and told her that I shouldn't be there because I was married.

At Creighton, the lecturer on nervous diseases was D. Douglas Singer who had studied under Sir William Gowers in London. His beautiful English fascinated me. I was the only one in his classes who passed.

When I went to Omaha to attend Creighton, I obtained an apartment near the college. I didn't know that the location was in a rough part of town. Our apartment was on the third floor. My dear friend May Ryder lived with me to help care for Nellie. We had not been there very long before May observed that many men visited our landlady. It was difficult for me to think there was anything out of the way, for she seemed respectable. I went down to her quarters to borrow something and a man was sleeping on her bed. It turned out that he was procuring patronage for her. The only women of that kind I had ever heard about lived in a little cottage on the outskirts of our county seat. Back of the cottage lot was a high board fence. I always wondered why the board fence, but after there were inside toilets the fence was taken down. The very next day I went in search of another apartment and secured an entire house so that I wouldn't need to be interested in my neighbors.

The winter was very cold, thirty-two degrees below zero. The pipes in the house froze and burst. I called the agent and he said I should pay to fix them because I lived there. In my inexperience I paid that bill, some forty-five dollars.

One day May, after reading a letter from her mother, asked me if I were rich today or very poor? Then she said that her mother thought I should buy May a coat for all she was doing for me. I was not stingy, but it had never occurred to me to pay her anything. We went downtown and I bought her a fine coat. We had both of us lived all our lives without money. It was educational for both of us and we were learning in many ways. She had spent a winter with me in Herndon too. All my life I have had such devoted friends.

At the end of my study at Creighton, I decided to take my child and go on vacation to the 1905 Lewis and Clark Centennial Exposition in Portland, Oregon. I knew nothing of any place except the Middle West and as we crossed the great sagebrush part of the West I wondered how people could live there. The landscape seemed dreary with only Lombardy poplars around the homes, peculiar trees with limbs clinging close to the boll. I have always preferred spreading elms. Then, at Salt Lake, little boys came alongside the train with big black cherries to sell, such cherries as I had never seen.

When we got as far as Hood River, the evergreen trees began to appear and the atmosphere became moist and cool. Here and there the vine maple showed its autumn coloring, though it was only August. Portland, Oregon, was a place of wonderful enchantment: the drizzly atmosphere, evergreens, blue hills, ferns, and clear streams. In the Middle West, the streams are all roily.

After arriving, I secured a room on Willamette Heights where I rested until ten o'clock the next morning. Nellie and I then went to the fair. I put a harness on her to keep her near as we wandered the fairgrounds. At two o'clock in the afternoon, we went back to our apartment where I put her down for a nap.

According to Mary's daughter Nellie, Nellie got out of her harness at one point to watch the monkeys and got lost. Mary found her after a panicky search.

After the fair we went to Long Valley, Idaho, to visit my sister May, Mrs. Maynard Loomis. My brother-in-law, Maynard, met us at Council, Idaho, as there was no railroad into the valley. On the way to the valley we had to sleep one night in the mountains among heavy timber. The next morning Maynard bent a pin, tied a string to it, and fastened it to a willow pole. As fast as he could throw it into the water he caught little mountain trout. He caught twenty-seven fish in no time at all. It was all like a fairyland to me.

My folks intended to take me south to Caldwell where I could board a train back to the Midwest, but somehow they didn't get their farm work organized as early as they had intended and there was snow in the valley and heavier snow in the mountains. The first night after leaving my sister's we had to camp on the side of a mountain. Maynard gathered fir boughs and placed them on the snow inside the tent and we made our beds on top. Then we went to bed wearing all our clothes. I curled my body around Nellie to keep her warm. I suppose she was the only one who slept at all as the cold came through the fir boughs, the bedding, and our clothing. We spent a miserable time trying to sleep. Maynard got up at four o'clock in the morning and built a big campfire, then we all got up to stand around the fire and tried to thaw out. He made coffee and fried bacon and potatoes which helped warm us.

The roads in the mountains were narrow and there were few places where one could pass another wagon.

Fortunately, not many were on the road. I finally boarded the train at Caldwell.

On the eastbound train I thought of my sister and her family, how they had gone to Idaho in 1902 just before Doctor died. Maynard filed on land in Long Valley and told how beautiful the valley was at the time with wild grass up to the horses' bellies. It was a valley several miles wide, with the north fork of the Payette River flowing through it. There was plenty of timber along the river and on the valley's eastern and western mountain slopes. At the head of this valley were the beautiful Payette Lakes. For the most part, the land was still government-owned and just waiting for homemakers to file on it. There were both sheep and cattle ranches. Maynard pointed out a corral where sheep men had shot twenty head of steers while the owners were nearby in a log house. The cattlemen didn't dare come out at the time, as they were unarmed.

May and Maynard had four children: Bernice, Clarence, Floyd, and Alvin. They had very little to start with, but out of native timber they built a one-room house. The first winter they went through terrible hardship, unaccustomed as they were to such deep snow. They were also late in getting the roof on their cabin. It was necessary to keep supplies on the floor, but the spring thaw brought water into the house and forced them to carry remaining supplies into the loft. The second summer they milked a few cows and my sister made cheese. With many bachelors and sheepherders in the county, there was a ready market for all she could make. The summer I was there they sold six hundred dollars worth of cheese.

They had much of their land under cultivation. The

two oldest boys helped Maynard while the girl helped
May. By 1909, they were milking thirty-two cows, sep-
arating the milk, and selling the cream. It was easier
than making cheese.

A Topeka Practice

After finishing school at Creighton, Mary felt it was premature to move west. Instead, she followed opportunity and started a medical practice in a familiar midwestern city. She was still involved with August Kleint at this time, though there is no record of the relationship in this period.

After graduating from Creighton in 1905, I located in Topeka, Kansas. Then I sent for my mother and Captain Barrett. Captain was a fine contractor and builder and I wanted him to build me a house. He planned it and it was like a hotel with twelve rooms. My mind was not mature enough to realize that I didn't need such a large house. It stands out near Washburn College today and is still beautiful after forty-seven years. The house had two stairways, front and back. The front stairway had two landings. The living room had a fireplace and floors inlaid with woods of different colors. Captain partitioned off a room near the kitchen and insulated it with charcoal for an icebox. Twice a week I put a hundred pounds of ice in it. To me the whole house was a wonderful creation.

Mary's mother had met Captain Barrett in Nebraska while he was constructing a local Christian church.

I belonged to a women's club in Topeka and some of the members seemed obsessed with the amount of money one had. They had the idea that if one man had two dollars and another only one, the man with two dollars was superior to the man with only one. I suppose the size of my house gave me a certain social standing, though I never really thought that was where my real worth lay. A man's value lies in his character or what he does with his talents.

The house was in a fine location for a home, but too far from the center of town to build a large practice. I wanted to live with my office, to have a home for my daughter. I have always lived with my office.

I rented a room in the house to a young medical student, Hubert Callahan, who often took Nellie out for a ride in her wagon. I almost made him one of the family. He had dark, curly hair that he hated. He made it sopping wet, then jammed his hat down over it, hoping it would come out straight when he took the hat off.

One spring Hubert came home from medical school with the bones of a skeleton they had finished dissecting. The bones had not been cleaned well and he said he planned to build a fire in my back yard and use an old boiler to cook all the flesh off them. I informed him that he was going to do no such thing, that he should take them right back to the medical college and finish his work on them there. He said all right, that he would, but instead he took the bag of bones and hid them in the loft of my neighbor's barn. He didn't tell the neighbor anything about it.

After a few weeks the neighbor smelled an odor in the barn, but it was several more before he climbed to the barn loft and discovered the bones. Of course, he thought that someone had been murdered and the murderer had hid the bones there. The poor man was in great distress for fear he'd be accused of the crime.

He called the neighbors and the minister of the church to which he belonged. They all met in his back yard and were contemplating calling the police. Hubert was in my barn at the time and heard them talking. He came running into the house and said, "Doctor, they found those bones. I didn't take them back as I agreed, but hid them in the neighbor's barn loft. What shall I do?" I said, "You go at once and tell him that they are your collection." He said, "Oh, Doctor, I am afraid to tell him."

Then I went out to the place where the men were huddled and told the neighbor what it all was. You could see the relief on the faces of the men. My neighbor thought about it a minute and then said, "Tell Hubert I don't think much of it."

The next year, Hubert went to Northwestern Medical in Chicago. He later graduated and visited me in Oregon before he began to practice. He located in Tulsa, Oklahoma, and built a fine practice as a specialist in urology.

Each summer after I had moved to Topeka I still went out to Rawlins County and practiced medicine. There was always plenty of cases. I usually stayed at the hotel in Atwood and left Nellie with friends. From there I took the train to Herndon and a livery team to make my calls. One evening after I had boarded the train to go back to Atwood and as the train pulled out of the station about eight o'clock in the evening, a great black cloud rose from the northwest. We had gone some two miles when the storm struck and I know that the train went only a few feet after that. The train included freight cars, with one coach for passengers on the back.

The wind, rain, hail, and thunder made a tremendous roar and were overwhelming. One could see nothing except the flashing lightning. I was the only woman on the train. I held my medicine case up to my shoulder to keep the hail off because the storm had at once blasted out the windows of the coach. The men were walking up and down the aisle like caged lions. I thought that someone would be killed, but I also thought that if I kept still I might get out alive. I huddled in the seat, unconscious that hail and water covered my feet. Then the storm passed, leaving its devastation.

The storm knocked the glass out of the engine room, cutting the engineer's face. The storm blew the tops off two boxcars and all the windows on the north side of the coach. There had been a wheat field beside the stopped train, just ready for harvest. Now the ground was bare and a little tree that stood there was stripped of leaves and even bark.

It was down a grade back to Herndon, and the engine was dead. The conductor stood on the back end of the coach with a lantern to see that there were no bridges out as we slowly backed the train down to Herndon. At the depot I sewed up the engineer's face, then waded in water in the street up to my knees to get to the hotel. Once there I was unable to sleep because of the ordeal. The men on the train told me they had never seen such nerve in a woman. I had made no outward emotional demonstration, but I had felt plenty.

Another time on the train to Herndon from Atwood, a great black cloud hung over the east. Arriving at Ludell, halfway between Atwood and Herndon, the trainman stopped to inquire as to the condition of the roadbed. The section foreman had just gone over the road and said it was okay; however, as we started, the engineer noticed that the bridge over a deep canyon was trembling. The canyon was full of running water that reached up to the bridge. Due to the downpour up the canyon, he stopped the train as the front wheels were on the approach to the bridge. We stayed there the rest of the night and in the morning, when the water receded, we saw that the bridge's underpinnings were gone. If we had not stopped, we would have gone into forty feet of water. Some of the men on that train trip said I was a hoodoo, as bad luck followed me. I suppose if I had lived a hundred years earlier they would have tried me for witchcraft.

Back in Topeka, one night after retiring, a friend called me to come at once to see a neighbor who was in a dying condition. When I arrived, all the neighbors had with great difficulty gotten the man into bed and were standing around while the wife sobbed. I asked the man where his pain was and he replied that he had no pain. The only condition I observed was that he was bathed in perspiration. His wife said he had mown the lawn before going to bed and that he had done some kind of manual labor in the heat of the afternoon. He had complained of being very tired and then went to bed early. She was awakened and found him huddled in a corner of the room, struggling and making terrifying sounds as if someone were strangling him. It was too dark for her to see and she began to scream, which brought in the entire neighborhood. Her husband was normal when I arrived and I assured them all that it had only been a nightmare.

While I lived in Topeka, I heard through a friend—a traveling man from Michigan—of a boy named Arthur whose mother had died when he was very small. He had lived with an aunt in Oregon until he was fourteen years of age, then ran away and finally became stranded in Michigan. In my inexperience, I thought I might be able to do something for him and sent him money for trainfare. The morning he arrived he had no baggage and said it had gotten lost on the way; that he had checked it, but when he arrived the baggage man could not find it. He said that the baggage man would look it up.

Mary's daughter Nellie maintained that Arthur was, in fact, the son of Mary's stepfather Captain Barrett. The Captain had several sons by a previous marriage.

I bought him a complete outfit of clothes and books for school. He went to school during the week, but on Saturdays I gave him carfare to go to the depot to see if they had found his suitcase. Each time he came back and said they hadn't found it yet. Each Saturday for a month he brought back the same information.

Finally Mother said, "Mary, I don't believe he had a suitcase and I'm going down with him when he goes again and see for myself." Mother went and at the depot Arthur eluded her by saying he had to go to the restroom. When he came back he said they had told him they were still looking for it. Mother was disillusioned and told me I better go see for myself. I just couldn't believe he was deceiving us, but I went to the depot anyway and asked about the suitcase. They sent me to the head baggage man and he said, "Well, the boy must have the checking ticket. You bring that in and we'll find the suitcase." As soon as he said that, I knew there was no suitcase.

When I got home, Arthur was busy cleaning Nancy's harness. I called him into my office and told him I wanted the truth. He hid his face and then said he'd been ashamed to tell me that he didn't have a suitcase.

The traveling man, a Gideon, had introduced him at the Y.M.C.A. After that, I gave him money to go to the Y every Saturday evening. After we learned the truth of the suitcase, Mother began to doubt that he even went to the Y and persuaded me to call there to find out. They told me he had been there but once, when the salesman from Michigan had introduced him.

At the Christmas vacation Arthur told us he had landed a job clerking. He left my house every morning and came home every evening, always bringing with him some kind of food, meat or groceries, and saying he had bought them with his own money. I was pleased at how he seemed to be doing. At Christmas he gave Nellie and me gifts. Everything seemed to be going along just fine until two weeks after Christmas when a letter came addressed to him. It was not sealed, so I took the liberty of reading it. It was from a downtown merchant telling him that if he didn't come and pay for the articles he'd bought, they would have him handled at once. I sealed the letter and when he came from school I gave it to him. At once he became excited and said he had to leave Topeka right away. He wouldn't tell me what was in the letter but went upstairs to his room and turned on the gas.

Mother said, "Let him kill himself. It will be good riddance." I didn't feel we should do that. I called a neighbor who went up to his room to have a talk with him. He had the gas on, but he also had a window open. He confessed that he had never had a job but had gone away every morning so I couldn't make him work. He said, however, that he'd be good now and do what I wanted him to do.

The grocer sent me a bill for all the things he'd been buying and charging to me. I noticed that he had also been buying candy for the girls at school. I finally sent him to live with his sister in the East, but no sooner had he arrived there than he was writing to come back, begging for one more chance.

By then, I was getting ready to go west. I had intended to settle in Boise, Idaho, to be in a larger place and closer to my sister May. It was 1909 when I rented a boxcar to ship my goods and horses.

When I moved to Topeka, I took a beautiful black mare, Nancy. I don't think I ever drove her downtown in Topeka, but a man once came out and offered to buy her. Nancy had a month-old colt and a yearling. I put the horses in one end of the boxcar and the household goods in the other. Arthur, who was back now, had been doing well and I let him ride in the boxcar to take care of the horses.

Long Valley

Mary anticipated settling in Idaho to be close to her sister May. The prospect of being near family members was comforting to her as her relationship with August Kleint was coming to a close.

When I arrived in Boise, it was so hot I felt I might drop dead. As soon as the boxcar arrived with my possessions, we hitched Nancy to her buggy, put the household goods in storage, and started for Long Valley. The first night we made it to Starr where we camped. As I remember it, there was no hotel. We just made our beds on the grass and cooked over the campfire. As we traveled, we tied the yearling to the buggy, but the colt followed by itself.

The second night we camped at Horseshoe Bend where the river enters a canyon. The third night we camped at Smith's Ferry, then made it to my sister's the next day. Today on a very fine road they make that little drive with an auto in about two hours. As I look back, it seems like quite an adventure to have made such an excursion with a sixteen-year-old boy, my little seven-year-old daughter, and a horse and two colts.

Another of my sisters and her family moved to Long

Valley later and filed on a piece of land, as did my
mother and stepfather. I soon bought four acres and
Captain Barrett again built a house for me. In late summer, May's husband Maynard advised me to buy a
quarter of beef. I did and we hung it on the north side
of the house. It hung there all winter or until we ate
it up. When we wanted some, we simply sawed off a
cut and cooked it. I bought cream and butter from my
sister.

The snow was wondrous as it made the trees bend
down with its weight. It was forty below zero, but the
men worked in their shirtsleeves pitching feed to the
cattle. Maynard and May were milking thirty-two head
of cows. Their children got up at four o'clock in the
morning and did the milking, then went in a sled six
miles to school at Roseberry. It seemed to me they
never went to bed before ten o'clock at night. They had
to have all their chores done before then.

The snow came early and was four and a half or five
feet deep, no place I thought for a woman to practice
medicine. I was discouraged and thought I would go
back to Kansas.

Meanwhile, Arthur helped with the milking to pay
for riding to school with the other children, but the arrangement dissatisfied him. He was almost seventeen
and obtained a job at Van Wyck, a town northwest of
Cascade that today lies under Cascade Lake, a
manmade reservoir. The merchant who hired him liked
him very much. When he had worked there a month or
more he told the merchant he had fallen heir to an eight
thousand dollar estate and would like to borrow enough
money to go out and settle it. On the strength of this
story, the merchant and two other men went security for

him at the bank and he obtained one hundred and fifty dollars. He came home the week before he left and wanted Nellie and me to leave the valley. I tried to find out why he was leaving, but he wouldn't tell me. We knew nothing of his borrowing the money until he had gone.

Mother suggested that I go to Oregon to the Willamette Valley to see if I could find a better place to practice medicine. Maynard, his brother, and a Mr. Blankenship were going to Lebanon, Oregon, to investigate and Mother thought I should go too.

At this time, Mary had taken the Idaho state examination to practice medicine, but did not pass. Discouraged by the exam results, the cold weather, and still under some stress related to her second marriage, she decided not to remain in Idaho to retake the examination.

I traveled with Maynard and the others to Lebanon, borrowed some medical books from Dr. Joel Booth, and went out into the country to bone up for the state board medical examination. There were one hundred and thirty-five prospective doctors who took the examination at the time and two were women. I think only thirty-six men passed, but both women passed. They caught one man cheating, handed him his examination fee back, and dismissed him. The examination took place July 3–5. Then I went back to Idaho where I had left Nellie with my mother. It was the last of August when I was notified that I had passed the Oregon state medical boards.

Before leaving Idaho for Oregon, my sister May gave

me a dog that was part collie and part St. Bernard. "Buster" was white and yellow and weighed ninety-five pounds. The Loomis boys wanted to keep him, but when they tried to use him with cattle and yelled at the cattle, Buster thought they meant him and he tucked his tail and headed for the house. May gave him to Nellie and we made him a part of our family.

One day Nellie brought a kitten home from school in her lunch bucket and was very pleased with it. When she came in she said, "Oh, Mama, I've got a kitty and it's a mama kitty." Anyone knows about female cats, but I let her keep it. She wanted to have Buster and the cat eat together, but Buster had other ideas about it and went out to his doghouse, an old piano box. There he sulked the whole day. When I tried to coax him to eat, he just turned his face away and pouted.

In the evening, I wanted him to go with Nellie to my sister's house which was several hundred yards through the woods. At last, he came out of his house, wagged his tail, and went. After that, he and the cat ate together, and when the snow got deep he often lay on a snowdrift with the cat curled up on top of him.

Leaving Long Valley on the way to Oregon we went through Lardo (now a section of the town of McCall). There we heard that Arthur had a big roll of bills and was posing as a traveling man from Salt Lake City. I contacted Mother to ask her to call the merchant Arthur worked for and tell him that he had money, and that we didn't know where he had gotten it. The merchant said, "Oh, Arthur is all right. He'll be back in three weeks."

My stepfather, Captain Barrett, had gone into the Civil War a private and come out a captain. We always called him Captain. After the war, he reenlisted and

served in Texas for some months. When he filed on a
piece of land in Long Valley, Idaho, he was allowed the
retirement income he had earned in the armed services.
He and Mother built themselves a little house on their
land and lived there until they received their patent. The
patent was signed by William Howard Taft in 1912. I
bought the land in Idaho they had recently proved up
on, that they might have money to build a house in Lebanon where we all intended to settle.

That fall they went to Lebanon, stopping in Weiser,
Idaho, on the way. While at a store making a purchase,
the merchant remarked on the Captain's military button
and hat. He asked him where he had served, from what
state, and in what company. When Captain told him his
name, regiment, and company, the merchant looked at
him and said, "My Captain." Then he fell on Captain's
shoulder and wept. After all those years! They had
plenty to discuss.

Captain Barrett was of Irish descent with all the char-
acteristics of the Irish: witty, energetic, full of pepper,
and quick-tempered. He always called Mother "Dearie."
At every meal he always ate the last meal's leftovers.
Invariably, he remarked, "Some folks keep a dog to eat
the leftovers, but Dearie keeps me." He died in 1928 of
a diabetic gangrene. We wanted to put him in a hospital
but Mother refused, saying she intended to take care of
him. It seemed to me he was slowly dying for that last
six months he lived. He was always sending for me to
come from Salem. I have no idea how many trips I
made. I was always running over there to see Mother
anyway, and after she died it was a matter of great comfort to me that I had done so much for her. She did all
she could for me when I was struggling to get an edu-

cation, and it wouldn't have been possible for me to neglect her when at last she needed me. Mother died in 1935 at eighty-seven years.

Those last years she had a gentle old soul keep house for her, a Mrs. McPharen who lived to be over one hundred years old. Mother also had a cousin, Henry Friday, who had come from Deadwood to visit her. Instead of making a visit, he just stayed on. We called Mother's house "The Old People's Home." They were very content, read the newspapers, and played Chinese checkers. After she died, Henry Friday lived with my youngest sister, Mrs. Nellie Ginther, until he died. Before he died, he asked Mother's girls if they would bury him beside Mother. And there he lies, the Captain on one side and Cousin Henry Friday on the other. After Mother's funeral, a man remarked to me, "I never saw an old lady who had as many friends as your mother."

The house the Captain built for us in Long Valley, Idaho, was accidentally burned to the ground after I left. The neighbors said two men had gone into it and spent the night. The next morning it was discovered on fire. The tragic part was that I carried no insurance, a bitter lesson learned the hard way.

The Canaga family included five children, oldest to youngest: May, Ben, Mary, Ida, and Nellie. May was born in Michigan and the four other children in Nebraska. Mary and Ida were playmates. Nellie, the youngest, idolized May, the eldest.

Before Mary's daughter Nellie died in 1993 she provided several sketches of Mary's sisters. Mary's brother Ben (1872–1927) was estranged from the sisters because of a dispute over Elias Canaga's estate.

Here is a paraphrase of Nellie's descriptions of the sisters and their families:

IDA *(1875–1960) wanted a girl but had a boy. When she was pregnant a second time, Mary was also pregnant. Mary had a girl and Ida said, "Mary always gets what she wants." Ida's second child was a boy, but it was months before anyone knew she had had a baby at all. She was so mad that the second child wasn't a girl that she didn't tell anybody.*

Ida talked as if she were perpetually mad. Her husband, John Miles, laughed all the time; he was a glad hander, politician, and joke teller. He was a county recorder for many years where they lived in Elwood, Nebraska, east of McCook. Later, they moved south of Salem, Oregon, but John got so homesick they finally moved back to Nebraska.

When John died, Ida, in her late fifties or sixties, moved back to Oregon and remarried. She dyed her hair. Ida's children were Jay, Walter, and John Jr. (Dick). Jay and Walter were named after Mary's husband "J. Walter."

Ida always had a great opinion of herself; she thought she knew everything. But she was funny because she didn't know it all, and was crazy. She exercised all the time to keep her form and was slender. She was up at the crack of dawn and went around exercising, burping, and rattling pans (to get everybody else up; she didn't like anyone to sleep too late).

Someone once told her she was lucky to have a sister for a doctor and she said, "Oh, I don't go to her, I go to a good doctor." Mary once pulled Ida's teeth and was about to get the deadener when Ida said, "Oh, no, just pull them!"

She was active to the end and died while sitting at a table doing her income taxes; she was a hard worker who maintained all of John's records.

MAY *(1870–1944) shared food and clothing and was hospitable, but never lent money to anyone, family or otherwise. When Captain Barrett was ill, May took care of him for Mary and her mother Ellen. Mary and Ellen paid for May's help with checks, not cash, to make sure there was a record of payment. When Ellen died, May took charge and divvied things up, but ended up with almost everything. She could manage everything to her benefit in one way or another. It wasn't for sentimental reasons either, because she sold it all, except for Ellen's silverware which she gave to Ida. Ida gave it away later as a wedding present to Aunt Nellie.*

May's children were Bernice, Floyd, Clarence, and Alvin. May doted over her youngest, Alvin. He was sickly, a puny start, and premature. He became husky in his late teens. He married Alma, known in the family as "The Flapper" because she loved to dance and wear low-waist dresses. Alvin was a happy person and not a kidder like his brother Clarence.

When I stayed with May and Maynard, May had Alvin—who was then eight years old—sleep with me. I was fifteen years old. I was embarrassed, of course, at the loss of my privacy and, you know, at having a boy in my bed.

NELLIE *(1882–1969) and her husband Perry Ginther lived in Nebraska for many years, then moved to Idaho where Perry ran a sawmill near Poison Creek with August Kleint. Perry originally wanted Maynard to go in with him but he declined.*

Maynard might not have thought Perry was a good businessman. Perry was a workaholic and used his body strenuously, but sometimes was taken advantage of. Mary thought Aunt Nellie was the sweetest person who ever lived.

Nellie's children were—youngest to oldest—Lois, John, Francis, Alice, and Ruth. The kids were a pack. John was often into mischief. Nellie once whipped John because he was eating fruit she had been drying for the winter. Her son Francis was bashful and studious and sometimes exaggerated. Alice was likable and very religious. After growing up, she expanded her horizons and developed a great tolerance for the world. Lois was a fine musician. Ruth, the oldest, was a hard worker and stubborn, like Perry.

I tried to please Ruth but couldn't. One time during a meal she asked me, "Do you like the food?" I responded meekly, "Not very well."

Before marrying Perry, Nellie was a lively young girl who went to all the dances and functions. Perry was religious—a Sunday school teacher—and handsome. He had a mustache. Perry wouldn't talk to Mary when she delivered Francis because she had been "divorced." Mary said later that she had saved both mother and child when Francis was born.

When Perry's lumber business in Idaho did not succeed, he and Nellie left for Oregon. His old mill site is now under the waters of Cascade Lake. There were many lean years and Mary felt Nellie worked too hard. They cultivated a garden, an orchard, and berry patches. Perry built houses toward the end of his life and made enough money for Nellie to have retirement income.

Main Street Lebanon

Overall, this period saw a strong rebound in Mary's sense of humor. With license now to practice family medicine in the state of Oregon, she was entrusted with many confidences. Her vignettes illustrate how she managed and appreciated them. Some reveal the thankless environment in which women doctors labored.

It was my intention to go on to Lebanon and from there look for a larger community in which to practice medicine. We, of course, took Buster, but we had to put him in the baggage car. When we boarded the train at Evergreen, Idaho—the nearest railroad station—Buster went right into the baggage car because he didn't know what it was. When we changed at Weiser to get on the main line, Buster refused to get on the other train and the baggage man finally picked him up and put him on. That was a terrible insult to him, but afterwards, at every division switchover, he jumped right off and on when we showed him where we wanted him. I think when he found out that we were traveling with him he was willing to obey.

When we got off the train at Portland we soon

110

learned that Buster had not relieved himself all the while he had been on the train. There on the tracks he had an enormous bowel movement, to our great embarrassment, but to the amusement of the trainmen. Also, when we were halfway uptown from the depot leading Buster on a leash, he stopped to urinate. The fluid ran across the sidewalk and down the gutter for several rods and everyone who passed gave a broad grin.

A rod is equal to five and one-half yards.

At Lebanon, I sent Buster to the country with a friend until I could get a place ready for him. But on the farm he killed a turkey thinking it was fair game and the woman he was staying with whipped him for it, after which he let the turkeys alone.

We boarded in Lebanon with a family from Idaho. We canned fruit as there was more of it than I had ever seen in my life. I was twenty-one years old before I had ever seen an apple growing on a tree in the Middle West. It seemed so wonderful to be where everything grew in such abundance.

After six weeks in Lebanon, I decided to go to Albany to look over the situation there. It was raining. I took Nellie with me and all day we walked around in the rain looking for an apartment to rent. The apartments looked so gloomy and dirty and Nellie kept saying, "Mama, let's go back to Lebanon where there's hills." When night came, we got on the train and went back to Lebanon where we stayed six years.

Lebanon had only board sidewalks then, and the intersections and streets were muddy. There were no sewers, so water stood everywhere in town. I stayed because I had friends there and was not yet bold enough to strike out to a larger town.

I rented a house on Main Street. The house was very old, but the location was right and I hung out my shingle. People went by and I heard them remark, "Dr. Mary C. Rowland, a woman doctor, well, well, well."

The first case I had was a little boy of ten or eleven. He came to me about half past eleven one night and woke me up to take care of his hurt finger. He had been in the bowling alley and a ball had hit his finger. He was crying and I asked him how he happened to come to me and he said, "Cause I know'd yore a woman, and you'd be careful." There you are. Many patients have come to me because they *know'd* I'd be careful. This little boy grew up and became the county sheriff.

Next a man wanted me to consult with a man doctor about his baby. It was a year old and had not been able to hold its head up. It was in the hospital in Albany where they had spent a lot of money, but the baby had not benefited. I called the other doctor and he said he had to go to the country, but for me to go and see the baby, which I did. The mother was half-distracted with constant care and worry over it. She said she could hardly change its diapers and the least touch to its gums made them bleed. I had never seen a case like it, but I had studied my books. They had been feeding it canned milk. I went home and called the other doctor and told him I thought the baby needed orange juice. He hung the receiver up on me.

In a few days, the father of the baby came to me and wanted me to take the case. He said that if I didn't take it they would get someone else. I told them that if they paid off their doctor they could have anyone they might choose. No doctor owns a patient, though some think they do. They paid the doctor and then came to me and I told them to go right on feeding the baby as they had, but add a teaspoonful of orange juice twice a day. On the second night, they came at three o'clock in the morning to tell me that the baby had been asleep all night and they were afraid it would die. It hadn't slept a whole night since they could remember. I told them to go home and let it sleep, that it needed that. In two months, you never would have recognized that child. The mother thought I could raise the dead.

The doctor who hung the receiver up on me must have been impressed with my diagnosis, for some years later he sent his daughter through medicine. You never see scurvy anymore as babies today receive a more balanced diet.

The next case was a woman who had been an invalid for seventeen years. She was treated all that time without any real help. She would feel fairly well and then she would develop a high temperature. Later, there would be a purulent discharge and she would feel better again until the time of a new attack. I made the diagnosis of an infected condition of the pelvis and took her to Albany. Dr. Russell Wallace and I removed the infected areas and she made a wonderful recovery. These cases put me on my way and soon I was as busy as any doctor in Lebanon.

I purchased a lot one-half block from Main Street on Sherman Avenue and built a good house with an extra room for my office. I never owned a horse after I came west as it was much less trouble to get a livery team when I needed to go to the country. One livery man always sent me out with the worst old nags and harnesses one could imagine. Once, some part of a harness broke and fell off and there I was twelve miles out in the country. I walked to a neighbor's house and he came out and mended it. After that, I refused to get my team from that livery man, but he came to my office inclined to quarrel because I patronized the other barn.

One man owned both barns and rented one to the man who sent me out with the nags. The other barn was for stabling horses and not livery. There was a lawsuit over the contract. The fellow who wasn't supposed to rent horses always gave me the best team he had, and if it was cold he put in hot bricks and plenty of blankets. I was subpoenaed to testify against him. I disliked the idea of testifying against him, but I had to tell the truth.

Later I had to testify against him again for shooting the town marshal. The marshal was George Loomis, a brother of my brother-in-law. The livery man got drunk one night and raised a great disturbance. George went to arrest him and he shot George in the thigh. George came to my office about midnight and called to me that the livery man had shot him and he thought the wound ought to be dressed. I dressed and came downstairs and called Dr. Jones to come help me. Dr. Jones was not a surgeon, so he stood by while I made an incision, cut out the bullet, and cauterized the wound. The femur was not fractured.

On the witness stand, the livery man's lawyer asked me to tell what had happened when the marshal came to my door. In telling the incident, I said *we* took the bullet out. Dr. Jones was sitting on the front seat of the court room and I did not want to embarrass him. Then the lawyer, thinking I presume, that Dr. Jones had taken the bullet out, said, "Now, just who took the bullet out?"

Then I said, "Well, Sir, I took the bullet out." Then the lawyer asked, "Isn't the marshal some relation to you?" I answered, "No, Sir, but I have known him all my life." We grew up in the same neighborhood in Red Willow County, Nebraska.

The hotel in Lebanon faced Main Street and the back end of the lot was directly across from my house. The hotel's outdoor toilet was on the back part of the lot. One day I heard a young woman screaming inside with the door closed. A man ran to the outhouse but hesitated to open the door, so I ran across to see if there was a murder. I opened the door without any hesitation. The poor girl was passing a tapeworm and thought her intestines were turning wrong side out. She was terrified out of her wits. I reassured her and told her what it was and that we would take care of it in time. There was in all some twenty-five feet of it.

I do not remember there being any paved roads in the Willamette Valley when I arrived in 1910. In the winter, the mud was deep, indeed, and in the summer the dust was almost as bad. Oregon has as fine roads now as can be found in any state.

Ralph Thom, a young man who worked for the Southern Pacific Railroad and belonged to the church I attended, often drove my team for me on my evening calls. We enjoyed these visits after his working hours, for we had much in common.

One spring everything looked beautiful except the roads which were muddy all the way, covered in hub-deep holes full of winter rain. Four miles out of Lebanon on our way to Lacomb we were talking and thinking of nothing serious, and the horses were walking because I was not in a hurry. The reins were hanging loosely when one wheel plunged into a deep chuckhole that startled the horses. They jumped forward breaking the singletree on one side, then jumped again forcing the tongue end down into the ground. At the horses' next lunge the tongue broke off and Ralph was pulled out at once, falling in such a way that his left leg stuck between the iron brace and the tongue. His body went down and turned backwards until his head was just in front of the wheel.

I didn't realize at the time that he was unable to get free and yelled for him to drop the lines. He was making a desperate effort to keep his head from hitting the ground. I always said that if the time ever came when I couldn't control my team I'd jump out, and that is what I did, alighting on my head and shoulders. As soon as I could get up I looked to see what had happened to Ralph. The horses went lunging down the road and turned off it to the right.

The horses dragged Ralph into a ditch full of water, then into a fence and stopped. After Ralph had extricated himself, the first thing he said was, "I want to go home to my mother." As bruised and battered as I was, I had to smile. I did not know how badly his backsides were mauled. It was a close brush with death for Ralph and I suppose I might have broken my neck when I jumped.

A family that I had first known back in Nebraska lived a short distance across a field. We made our way there and they outfitted Ralph as best they could while I phoned for another livery team to come and get us. The livery man admitted that he had known the left horse to be untrustworthy. The wonder of it all was that neither of us had a broken bone, and only plenty of bruises to keep us occupied for a couple of weeks. Meanwhile, in all the excitement, I forgot my destination.

Ralph said later that he didn't remember how we got home, or what happened to the team and buggy afterwards. He said he remembered getting out of bed the next morning and finding "not a square inch from my neck to my seat that was not black and blue from the beating I took." The runaway happened in 1912, some forty-two years ago.

While I was practicing in Lebanon, a man once cursed me. He sent for me to come to his house some fourteen miles east of town. His wife had given birth to their tenth child without an attendant and the baby was born at two o'clock in the morning. Following the birth she had a severe hemorrhage. It was five o'clock when he sent for me and seven o'clock when I arrived. Blood saturated everything in her room. She looked like a dead woman. I delivered the placenta and cleaned her up as best I could. I told her husband that she was in a bad way and should be taken to a hospital for proper treatment.

He then asked me what my bill was. I charged him twenty dollars and he started cursing me. He said, "Why did I ever call for a woman doctor in the first place?" I said, "You can pay me whatever you wish, but if you do not take care of your wife you will lose her." He said he'd attend to his own business and that I could attend to mine. That poor wife lived a year and died. I saw later in the paper that he also had died and left thirteen children. I knew he must have married again since the youngest child I knew was the tenth. He had gone about his community telling people that I killed his wife. I think people understood it all though, for I had a large practice in his neighborhood.

The young man who contracted to build my house let me know he did not want me to come about the house while he was working on it. I was amused about that order. He was willing to take a woman's money but not willing to have her supervise its spending. The house, built in 1912, looks as good today as it did then, though now is surrounded by business buildings.

A little woman who had moved from Lebanon to Corvallis after she married came home to visit with her mother. She was in the early stages of pregnancy and had a high temperature so they sent for me. I told her husband that the fetus was dead and that she should be curetted. He said that if she was pregnant he did not know where she had gotten it. I knew that what he inferred was pure scandal. He refused to have her curetted and let her lie there two days, delirious, until he finally consented for me to take care of her. I called another doctor to give the anesthetic. The husband said he wanted me to do the curetting and that he didn't want any "monkey business"! *Monkey business* with his wife in the condition she was in!

I made him pour the sterile water while I worked. I made up my mind that if he tried to interfere with me while I was working I would stab him with my scissors, but he caused no further trouble and she made a recovery. In a couple of years they separated due to his insane jealousy. There are so many things in life that one must take on trust.

One thing in my practice for which I take satisfaction is how few women have ever been jealous of me in view of the intimate association I have had with their families. I always watched that I not take advantage of or do something toward some other woman that I would, myself, have resented.

Only one woman was ever jealous of me that I know of and it happened this way. At Lebanon, one night after the Eastern Star meeting, we were having a supper or plate dinner. The superintendent of the paper mill filled his plate and came and sat by me. He was not well acquainted with me and it was only a friendly gesture, but his wife across the room got up and came over to him, snapped her fingers, and told him to give her the keys to the house, that she was going home. The poor man said, "Well, wait awhile and I'll go with you." Again she snapped her fingers at him and said, "Give me that key." What a woman! He took his plate over to the table and left like a whipped dog. I never saw him again. I wondered what kind of life he must have led, with a woman who had no more trust in him than that. Jealousy is one of the great evils in this world.

The roads in Kansas and Nebraska run along section lines and it's not difficult to find any home where you might want to go. But in Oregon, in the early days, they meandered along with the contour of the land. It was with great difficulty that I learned to negotiate some of them. Often I had to depend on the descriptions that women gave me to find their homes. Did you ever ask a woman to describe a road to you?

One woman called me to come to her house some twelve miles from Lebanon, and in describing the road told me to turn off another road and follow it by the east bank of the Santiam River. I followed her directions and eventually came up against a sawmill directly across the road. The river on one side and a cliff on the other blocked me on a narrow road. The men working at the sawmill said the road had not been used for more than two years.

I was driving a small team from the livery barn and they were not very gentle. In trying to turn, one of them got its back under the tongue and both horses began lunging. The buggy came up on two wheels and I was in great danger of being thrown into the river. There was no time for the mill men to come to my rescue so I lashed those horses with all my might and they made haste to get unscrambled. They made the turn and away we went back down the road at a gallop to find a better route.

Another time I followed directions that took me to the first road past the Berlin corner. It was in the middle of the night and the only thing I had to depend on was the directions. The family had forgotten to mention that the first road led into their meadow. They should have indicated that I was to turn onto the second road. I came up against a very high, woven wire fence, but could see the house light across the field. I tied my team there, took my medicine case, and climbed the fence thinking the man of the house could go out and bring my team around later.

After I climbed the fence, I began to wonder what they kept in such a high enclosure. I skirted the fence thinking that if it were some dangerous animal I could hear it coming and would try to climb back out. However, I heard nothing, but finally reached a canal full of running water. I searched about and found a small pole across it and managed to hold my balance until I was across. When I came to the other side of the high enclosure, I climbed out again and was soon at the home of my patient. They said they were sorry that they hadn't thought about the road to the meadow. They told me later that they had kept the high fence to enclose a cross bull, but had recently sold him, for which I truly felt grateful.

I ministered to my patient and, it being late, they invited me to stay the rest of the night. They put me in their spare bedroom which was unheated. Late that night the husband of my patient came into my room and tucked the covers around me. I pretended to be asleep, but in reality was paralyzed with fright. His behavior indicated that he might somehow be mentally disturbed. Subsequent to this incident, I learned that his behavior grew progressively more unusual until he went insane. He later died in the state mental hospital.

At one time, I had another female medical competitor in Lebanon. No one knew anything about her except that she said she had come from Canada. She hung out her shingle as Dr. "so and so" and announced that she could, by diet, make a person one or two inches shorter or taller as necessary. Everyone seemed dissatisfied with their height judging from the patronage she received. She was very soon doing a vast business, but her patients eventually grew disillusioned and business fell away.

Her office and home were on the upper floor in the former post office across from the hotel. A light one night caught the attention of a young man who lived in the hotel. He looked out and saw fire and smoke issuing from the building where the woman lived. He dressed hurriedly, ran across the street, and found her at the head of the stairway with her trunk packed, waiting for someone to take it down.

The firemen put the fire out before the building collapsed and said they found rags saturated with coal oil stuffed between the plaster and outside walls. The woman carried fifteen hundred dollars in insurance though she had about three hundred dollars' worth of equipment. The cashier of the bank who had written the insurance paid her the full amount before she left on passage to the South Pacific.

The gossip was that she had set the fire herself. I felt outraged that anyone would accuse her of such a thing and before she left I went to see her thinking that if she knew what people were saying she would do something to clear herself. In speaking with her she would not look me in the face, but said she had not done it and believed someone else had. I asked her who would do such a thing and she said possibly her enemies. I asked who her enemies were and she said she did not know.

Throughout my years of practicing medicine there were occasional frauds. One man came to Lebanon claiming that he had a fluid that could cure cancer and that he could put patients to sleep by suggestion. Rumor of his special powers went all over town and sounded wonderful to hopeless patients. One of our local doctors had a patient suffering from a recurring cancer of the breast. Her husband mortgaged their home to pay the local doctor and this famous "specialist." They invited me to witness their operation and paid me nothing. The specialist asked me not to come until he had the patient's nerves composed. I arrived, however, before he expected me and saw he was just ready to give her a narcotic hypodermic. I told the patient that he was a fraud, but they paid no attention to me for I was only a woman.

I then watched the *operation* that consisted of cutting into the cancerous tissue. Without sterilizing his hands or wearing rubber gloves the specialist then felt around in the wound. The patient moaned and seemed unable to keep from screaming. But the specialist kept repeating over and over, "Now, go to sleep. You are in God's hands." Finally he asked me if I wouldn't mind giving her a little ether. Of course, I was glad to do so. Our local doctor helped him as he poured a brown liquid into the wound and remarked that it would cure her. In a short time, the patient died and before she died she said, "Little did we think that Dr. Rowland knew more than that specialist."

Our local doctor could not have been so ignorant. To me it was no more than robbery. We have laws now to protect people from such charlatans. Gertrude Stein wrote, "Is money money or is money money?" Money is money when you earn it, but when you get it by chicanery it is pollution.

As secretary of the medical association in Lebanon, Mary once wrote to the state about a doctor in a nearby county who was dispensing narcotics to addicts. The state wrote back that action was being taken and that the doctor's license had been suspended.

An Italian named Petro, who had been in the community for many years, was in an accident and suffered a broken back. The accident commission was giving him a pension for he had several children, and I delivered his wife of another one. For some reason, right after the baby came his pension was delayed. He made his way to my office terribly perturbed, thinking that, because he had had another baby, the commission had cut off his pension. The poor fellow didn't know how he was going to live. I reassured him that his pension would surely come in a few days. Soon he came to tell me everything was all right, that the pension had come.

Another family in town may be worth mentioning because they were very unusual. A predator took advantage of one of the daughters who was in a wheelchair. The mother was away from home at the time and the girl was going to have a baby. When I revealed the pregnancy to the mother, she remarked, "I don't feel too bad about it, for Maggie never has much pleasure in life anyway."

They moved away from town and I forgot all about them until some years later when I read in a local paper that the parents were appealing to the paper to help them get their daughters—twelve and thirteen years old—out of a local hospital. The authorities of the hospital refused to give them up for reasons of indigence. I investigated and found that the stepfather, who was later sent to a penitentiary, had been having sexual relations with the girls.

The family went on relief while the father served his term. The warden of the penitentiary, meanwhile, allowed some wards to go home for weekends, among them the stepfather. In due time, I delivered his wife of another baby and he remarked, "I told the warden it was unsafe to let me go home."

The Lebanon town drunk was not a bad man; in fact, he was a good workman when sober. He lived in discouraging conditions with his sister who was a bedridden drug addict. Periodically he would go on a bender, then get extremely depressed. When I was the city health officer he came to me and asked me to have the jail fixed up. He wanted a soft bed where he could sober up in comfort.

One night at midnight he came to my house and woke me to ask where he could find another doctor. I scolded him for bothering me. It was soon afterwards that he decided to commit suicide, taking his doctor and the druggist to the undertaker where he picked out a white casket. The two men dissuaded him from suicide, but about a year later in the summer he came home with a pint bottle of formaldehyde and announced to a neighbor woman that he was going to drink the bottle and end it all. He poured out a cup full, but the neighbor knocked it out of his hand. Then he picked up the bottle and drained it down his throat.

In his agony he ran outdoors screaming for a doctor. Someone sent for Dr. Miller who usually took care of him. The doctor, however, was ready to go to the country and did not believe the man had really taken the poison. He told the messenger that he would come when he got back from the country.

Finally, the town marshal went for Dr. Booth who didn't believe it either and said, "Let him drink it. It'll do him good." Dr. Booth wasn't really callous; I think he honestly didn't believe the man had taken the poison. At last, the marshal came for me and I thought maybe he had taken it so I went to see. I found him writhing on the grass in his front yard. When he saw me he pleaded for me to do something for him. I told the marshal to go and tell Dr. Booth to come at once and bring a stomach tube that we might wash his stomach and try to save the poor creature. Dr. Booth came immediately and when we began to get the poison out of his stomach the fumes were so strong we could hardly work with him. However, all our efforts were of no avail. He lived until the next morning, conscious to the last and in terrible agony.

Another unusual character in Lebanon was Ray Leonard who had come to Lebanon many years before with his father. They were shoe cobblers and lived quietly by themselves. When the father died, Ray wouldn't let the undertaker have anything to do with his father's body until he'd prepared it for burial. He was often seen going to the cemetery afterwards.

When Ray first came to town he and another man were rivals for a maiden lady who used a large ear trumpet. It was said that the two men almost dueled over her. Nothing came of the whole affair. One man moved away and Ray ceased to call on the lady. He lived in the back of his shop which became a rendezvous for men of the town who gathered there in the evenings to tell stories. Ray went hunting and fishing with these men, but always insisted on sleeping alone. As time passed, he became gray and looked quite old, complained of headaches, and often closed his shop at odd hours. Eventually, he began to wander about town at night and seemed disoriented. People who knew him and found him wandering would take him home. Finally, it became necessary to put him in the state hospital.

It is customary to strip each patient entering the hospital and give them a bath before they are given quarters. The hospital immediately discovered that Ray

Leonard, a nineteen-year resident of Lebanon, was a woman. After her secret was out, Ray made a rapid recovery and came back to Lebanon to live the rest of her life.

The authorities made her wear dresses, but she confided to her friends that she wore pants below her dress because her legs got cold. She told people that she was the oldest daughter in a large New England family and had grown up helping her father in the shop. After consulting her father they agreed she would do best to wear men's clothing.

Ray was quiet, industrious, and not given to controversy in the community. Back from the asylum she frequented the Christian Science Church, though always sent for me when she was ill. She always remarked, "Christian Science is all right when I'm well, but it ain't worth a damn when I'm sick."

Ray looked far more like a man to me than a woman. She would say, "Look at me, Dr. Rowland, do you think I have one feminine feature?" I had to admit that she certainly looked like a man.

Meanwhile, Ray's shop became poison to the men who formerly gathered there to tell tales. The doctor who cared for her all those years crossed the street to keep from speaking to her. And the men of town never ceased to ask the doctor why he had kept Ray's sex a secret. Men everywhere have their little jokes.

When people yelled into the maiden lady's ear trumpet that her old beau was, indeed, a woman, her remark was, "Why the old !@#*!"

After we had settled in Lebanon, we received a card from Arthur saying, "Why don't you write?" The card, mailed at Salem, had his picture on the back. It was the first we had heard anything of him since he had run away from Idaho. Soon we heard a rumor from Idaho that he was in the reform school at Salem. I wrote to the authorities there and they said there was no one there by that name. Then I sent the card I had received and they answered right away that Arthur was in the penitentiary.

It seemed that he and another fellow had gone to Dufur, Oregon, and bought a gallon of whiskey from a bootlegger. They were posing as U.S. marshals and threatened to turn the bootlegger in if he didn't pay them. If he paid them one hundred and fifty dollars, they said they would just ignore it. The bootlegger paid the sum, but grew suspicious and turned them in. They were both put in the penitentiary for two years.

Along February of the next winter, the two of them went before the governor and swore that the fellow with Arthur really thought Arthur was a U.S. marshal. On the strength of this, he was pardoned. I then received a letter from the chaplain telling me that, if I would stand sponsor for Arthur, they would parole him to me. I wrote right back, "No, Sir, I will have nothing more to do with Arthur. I already did all I knew to do for him, and he took advantage of my reputation to do people out of their money. I am done."

After he served his time he went to Tillamook and persuaded his cousin to give him another start, then took advantage of her too. She wrote me that after he left Tillamook he went to California and there married a girl whose father had a large ranch. He seemed to do fairly well until about the time his wife had a baby. His father-in-law sent him to the city to get the payroll money for the men who worked on the ranch and Arthur took the money and ran away. His father-in-law said he would have him taken care of if it were the last thing he ever did. He finally caught up with Arthur and had him sent to a California penal institution. It is now twenty-five years since I have heard anything further. No doubt he is serving time, or someone has killed him.

After I built my house in Lebanon, the neighbors told me of an old man who went about cleaning houses. I employed him and found him a wonderful character. Everyone called him Uncle Henry and he lived in an old barn at the back of the Presbyterian minister's home. He had partitioned off a room in the barn with old quilts, rag carpets, gunny sacks, and "what have you." He had a flattop wood stove for cooking.

Henry was seventy years old when I first met him, short in stature, and plump. His hair was like snow and he walked with a rolling gait as though the earth was a ship and he was forever adjusting his body to the heaving of the deck. He neither smoked nor drank. Often I saw him in some back yard beating rugs as if his life depended on it.

When conversing with him you knew he had traveled widely. He said he'd been seventeen times round the world on sailing vessels, round Cape Horn and the Cape of Good Hope. He related many incidents that he located in Africa, India, Australia, or other faraway places. He said he had stayed a long time in Australia (four months, a long time for Uncle Henry). He said he had walked the entire length of Ceylon and "preached the gospel" on the streets there or in people's homes.

He was born in Brighton, England, as Henry Lawrence and when eleven years old ran away because he didn't want to go to school. He had never gone back nor written a word home. He said his family was musical and his father a very fine musician. Henry had himself played the trombone.

Sometimes Uncle Henry disappeared for a year or two, then suddenly reappeared. He usually said he had been in California taking care of gardens, sometimes in Eureka. He never explained why he went away but some people suspected that he traveled somewhere to deposit money, perhaps Canada. No one really knew.

As the years passed, I was traveling more and more. The automobile brought many changes beginning in my years at Lebanon. For a long time after the Ford got onto the roads, the churches were almost empty. Men took to the highways and to the woods with their families, saying God was in the woods and in the mountains, along the streams, and at the seashore. Doctors were among the first to obtain some of the better autos.

At the medical banquets there was bragging about speed. One doctor said he had turned a corner on two wheels and on the straightaway went all of thirty-five miles an hour. One man, who drove a car for a time, then tried to drive a horse team again, almost killed his horses because they were so slow.

In 1916, I decided to get an automobile, but didn't like the idea of spending the money for a new one. A friend in Portland said he could get me a very good one for two hundred and fifty dollars. I sent the money and he made the purchase, then he and his wife brought it down to Lebanon. It was an old Model T Ford. You turned the gas on, cranked it, then you cranked it repeatedly until it started. Sometimes you had to spin the crank, almost an impossible task for me. Placed on the left fender was a little tank of Presto fluid that powered the lights. You turned the fluid on, then went to the front of the car, took the glass off the headlights and touched them with a lighted match.

My car was in generally poor condition and I had one blowout after another. Something went wrong with it every time I tried to go anyplace. It was wonderful, however, when it was going. I felt on top of the world when it was running properly. I had a sense of well-being.

Most people thought that way. The banker's wife, who was fond of me, complained of obscure pains in the region of the liver, but I was unable to diagnose her case and sent her to Portland to Dr. Coffee. Her son, a surgeon in Boise, came to Portland and neither Dr. Coffee nor her son could make a diagnosis. They finally made an incision and found she had cancer of the pancreas. She came back to Lebanon thinking she was cured. We never told her what her trouble was and her husband asked me what he should do if she lost faith in me because she didn't improve. I said we would cross that bridge when we came to it. Toward the last she had to have hypodermics several times a day and only allowed me to give them to her. She often said during those times, "When I get well, as I expect to, I'm going to get the finest automobile with all the newest gadgets and take you out for a ride every day."

Sometime after her death, her family, some friends, and Nellie and I drove up to Belknap Springs on the McKenzie River. My car had several blowouts on the way and a young man mended the tires. The others arrived ahead of us and had a tent pitched and a campfire ready for supper. It was inspiring to be there among the trees and the cool mountain air. After breakfast next morning, all the young people took off on trails and one

man went fishing, leaving me in camp with a disagreeable woman who flew up at me when I called her
"Auntie." "You don't need to call me 'Auntie,' for I am
not much older than you," she said. The woman seemed
to have cockleburs sticking out all over. Of course, I
hadn't the least intention of offending her, but it spoiled
everything for me.

To top it off, standing over a smoking campfire and
cooking in a drizzle was no fun. I thought to myself "I
just can't take it" and announced I was going home.
They tried to persuade me to stay, but I told them that
they could all stay as long as they pleased, that it was
no fun for me. I was not very mellow in those days.

I had driven only a few miles when I discovered that
the car wouldn't pull up the hills. I backed it up and
tried to make a run for one hill, but the engine died
again and again and I had to get out in the mud and
crank it. It was no use. There we sat in that miserable
situation, miles back to camp and no idea how far the
next house might be. I sat there contemplating, when
along came a young man leading a saddle pony. I
noticed a rope looped over the saddle horn.

He said the horse had only recently been saddle-
broken and had never pulled a pound in its life. Nevertheless, he tied the rope to the saddle horn and to the
car. It was something to see that little pony snake us up
the hill, snorting and groaning. We were all day going
fifteen miles, but made it to a friend's summer house on
the McKenzie before dark.

Lebanon had a Strawberry Fair each year and its time
was approaching. I decided to trim my Ford up and put
it in the parade. I wanted the druggist who was my part-
ner in a drugstore business to help me get it ready, but

he didn't offer assistance. My stepfather, Captain Barrett, put some timbers around it and made it look like a boat. I covered it with mosquito netting, then vine maple, hundreds of crepe paper poppies, and purple lupine trim. I drove the car and in the seat beside me were three little girls dressed in sailor suits. I draped an American flag around them.

The effect was quite pleasing. I didn't get a photograph of the car as after the parade I had to go at once to the country. When I came back, someone said to me, "Dr. Rowland, you got the first prize." I said, "Yes, I did," not believing a word of it. Shortly, someone else said the same thing. I went into the drugstore and the druggist told me it was so. Finally, I went and claimed the prize.

The next car I had was a Maxwell, not much better than my old Ford. It was flimsy and its vibrating broke the fenders. There were also large open holes in the floor near the gearshift. This caused some trouble on one trip from Albany to Salem in about three inches of snow. While coming down a hill I turned the ignition off and coasted. But when I went to turn the ignition on again the key had jiggled out and fallen through a hole in the floorboards. It was hopeless to try to find it in the snow. A friend was with me and I told her that the key was a straight piece of metal with two projections, and a substitute might start the car. She reached up under her dress and pulled out a corset stay. We split it into two pieces, then used it to start the ignition. You know the old saying, "Necessity is the mother of invention."

There was, formerly, an undertaking establishment in Lebanon operated by a man and his wife. The wife was a friend and she used to tell me about some of her customers. One woman came and asked how much it would cost to have her husband's body disinterred and cremated. He had been dead some years. The undertaker told her it would not cost much. The widow said she would think about it and went away. The undertaker began to cogitate on the matter and wondered just why she wanted to have her husband's body cremated. Had she poisoned him, or what? Then one day very soon the widow came again and ordered the body taken up and cremated, so the undertaker asked her just why she was going to do this. "Well," said the widow, "I found out that I could get a good price for the lot in the cemetery and I do so want an automobile."

In 1916, before I left Lebanon, a man from Portland came to my office and introduced himself. He was an old gentleman and had a decent appearance. He said he and some others were organizing a company to manufacture automobiles and were locating the factory at Gresham, near Portland. He talked me into putting one hundred dollars into it. I still have the certificate.

A year or so later when I had my office on Liberty Street in Salem, he came again and said that he and his partners were going to make moving pictures. They had organized a company for that purpose. The automobile and the moving picture industries were both young. It looked as though it would be a good thing to put some money into the picture business too. Anyway, he sold me another five hundred dollars worth of stock.

I was acting in good faith, but shortly after I moved into the Liberty Street building, a young man came to my office and introduced himself as the same man. He was much younger than the other man and I asked if he was his son. He didn't answer me at once, but tried to sell me some more stock in the moving picture business. I pinned him down to the question, "Are you his son?" Then he said he was not, but that the man had told him how to introduce himself.

I began to think there might be some kind of fraud, so I told the young man that if his overseer was trying to cheat a widow I certainly was going to have him taken care of. The young man went away and in a few days I received a letter signed by the older man saying that if I wanted my money back I could have it. Needless to say, I went to Portland that very same day to get my money, but he was out of town. I left his letter with a collector I knew and he went the following day and recovered the money for me.

A few years later, the entrepreneur died and one of the Portland papers gave him quite a eulogy, telling what an enterprising gentleman he was, to which I could testify, for he talked me out of a total of six hundred dollars, but with a little encouragement returned five hundred dollars. I never heard anything more of his auto company.

Before I left Lebanon, an incident occurred that I think helps explain why my husband always called me "The New Woman." When we had that little brush with Mexico in 1916, I went to Portland and tried to enlist in the Army.

Mexican political events from 1913 to 1917 involved a string of border disputes with the U.S. In 1916, soldiers of Pancho Villa shot eighteen American miners near Chihuahua City. Several months later, American troops under the command of General John Pershing,

*routed Villa's army following border raids by Villa
into Arizona and New Mexico.*

Dr. Marcellus told me they had never heard of such a
thing, that the Army did not take women. I didn't know
the first thing about the organization of an army and
was unaware that women were not a part of any army.

My relatives had fought in every U.S. war including
the Revolutionary War and my father together with
twelve of his cousins fought in the Civil War on the
side of the North. As I had no man in my family I
thought I should go. I know now how ridiculous it must
have seemed to everyone but me. I envisioned myself
riding a horse over the battlefield and giving first aid to
the wounded. Imagine my embarrassment when Dr.
Marcellus put it in the paper that Dr. Mary C. Rowland
from Lebanon had tried to enlist in the United States
Army.

But times change. My niece, Lois Ginther, enlisted in
the Second World War as a WAC. She graduated from
university with a music degree, then enlisted and
trained in Des Moines, Iowa, for the WAC band. She
was in Abilene, Kansas, when our Ike came back from
Europe at the end of the Second World War.

New York City

This chapter—not intended to follow the Lebanon chapter chronologically—records a trip that occurred while Mary lived in Lebanon. It is brief and the reader wishes for more. No sooner has she described the great city of New York and a few incidents there than she is back on a train bound for the West Coast. The chapter also imparts Mary's character through several letters.

In 1913, I decided to go to New York to do some postgraduate work. I had never been east of the Mississippi River and it was quite an adventure for me as I was going alone. I left Nellie with the Christian minister who had a little girl with whom she could play.

Buster was to stay at home and the druggist promised to take care of him. Buster got little attention from the druggist after I left, however, so he took up residence with the town marshal, Frank Richards, and went with him on all his calls.

Ralph Thom, who was with me when my team ran away, had a cousin, William Thom, who was an editor at a New York paper. Ralph had written him telling of my upcoming trip. Being a bachelor, he took me under his wing as soon as I arrived.

My trainfare cost one hundred and sixty-five dollars. At Detroit, I crossed over into Canada, visited Niagara Falls, and from there went to Albany, New York, where I caught a boat. The Henrich Hudson floated me down to New York City, past West Point which looked like a penitentiary. Always before when I went any distance I took a noisy train. On this trip along the river, the city seemed to float up like a beautiful dream.

A couple of rather unfriendly women on the boat told me they had reservations at a Y.W.C.A. near Union Square, but they didn't think I could get a room there unless I had it reserved. I didn't know the first thing about New York, but thought to follow them off the boat and see where they went. When they got on the streetcar I got on too, and when they got off I did too. I followed them into the Y.

The place seemed to be run by a couple of cranky maiden ladies. When they found I was from Oregon and had money to pay, they gave me a room saying that no one could stay more than four weeks. They let me stay six weeks, however. I suppose they had that rule to prevent girls from coming to the city and getting stranded.

In a letter dated July 14, 1913, to her sister Nellie, Mary describes her accommodations in the following tone, "I am rooming at the Women's Christian Association, which is a great place to stay. No men allowed, but as I do not care particularly for men, especially those I do not know, it makes it very nice for me."

The New York Post-Graduate Medical School I attended was within walking distance. Five days a week I attended lectures and clinics, and in between Mr. Thom took me to interesting places and lovely restaurants and theaters. He seemed to enjoy taking me about. It was all like fairyland and my head was full of it all.

The postgraduate school, then located at Second Avenue and 20th Street, eventually merged with New York University.

The most pleasing outing was to the American Museum of Natural History, but I also went to the Metropolitan Museum of Art, the Battery, the Bronx Zoo, Coney Island, and many other places. He knew his New York. One night at midnight he took me to see "The Bread Line." He told me that a man who owned a bakery gave away leftover bread every midnight. We watched as a file of old derelicts, not a woman among them, shuffled along until the bread disappeared.

In a note exuding mother love scribbled on New York Post-Graduate Medical School letterhead dated August 4, 1913, Mary wrote a quick note to her eleven-year-old daughter Nellie: "My Darling Baby, I am so homesick for you, dear, but you be a good girl and I'll be back as soon as I can. I am learning a lot of new things here at the school and hospital. I will send you some stamps in this letter so you can write to me often. Don't forget Mama and be a good girl. Write. A world of love for you, Baby.—Mama"

In the earlier letter dated July 14, 1913, to her sis-

ter Nellie she was more descriptive and lengthy, showing her amazement at technology changes and the fact that New York had fresh air owing to its oceanside location and the industrial switch from coal burning to electricity: "My Dear Sister Nellie: Well, here is your big sister in the second largest city in the world and the cleanest. Could you imagine a city with 5,000,000 people without smoke or telephone or telegraph wires? Well, New York is it. The wires are all underground. There is no soft coal burned in the city, and all the trains are hauled in by electric motors and . . . as many as 70,000 people enter and go out of the city every day. And these people are brought in and taken out underground under the Hudson River, as New York City is on an island. The streets are so clean and they look narrow, but only because the buildings are so tall. Most of them are many stories high, and, oh, the noise and roar and motion. Streetcars, autos, trucks, people going every way, and every day somebody gets in the way of something and is killed. They have tunneled under the ground for some of the streetcars, for some they have built elevated lines, and some run along the middle of the streets. A wonderful city and I am glad I spent my money to come."

It was a great surprise to me, after I crossed the Mississippi River on my way to New York, to see the enormous number of people. They seemed as thick as flies, and very few looked happy. How do people enjoy living in such crowded conditions when there is so much free air and such wide and open vistas everywhere in the West? I found so many who were vague about their geography. After I told one woman I was from Oregon, she said, "I had a friend go west once, but I don't know whether it was to Oregon or Wyomington."

I used to sit routinely in Union Square and watch people going home from work. One evening I counted them, estimating that 35,000 persons passed along that path in one hour on their way to or from some dirty hole-in-the-wall where they lived. They all seemed bent on merely staying alive. They lived out their sordid lives and hardly saw sunlight.

While 35,000 may be an exaggeration, New York writers such as Walt Whitman described the city before the turn of the century as having "numberless crowded streets" and "immigrants arriving, fifteen or twenty thousand in a week."

One evening I thought to go to a fruit stand and get some fruit as the next day was Sunday. Then I wouldn't have to go down for breakfast, but could lie in bed and rest. It was not quite dark, and as I passed a corner I noticed some men standing there. I bought my fruit and started back to the Y when one of the men detached himself and started to follow me. At first I thought that maybe he just happened to be coming in my direction, but he began to catch up with me. Then I thought maybe he was going to grab my purse so I changed it to the other hand. Then he said something to me. I never did know what he said, but suddenly I was so mad I could hardly see. I whirled on him and said, "Mister, you get going or I'll shove you in the gutter." He said, "Oh, excuse me madam, I've made a mistake."

He turned and hurried back away from me. I suppose any big city is full of such crums.

Another time, I went to cross a street where a policeman was standing in the middle directing traffic. I ran over to him but he acted highly indignant and said, "Madam, can't you see when a man has got his hand up?" I bustled up to him and sassed him right back, "Now, how would I know what a man means when he has his hand in the air?" He grinned and said, "You stand right here until I tell you to go." He knew I must have been a New York tenderfoot.

Once in Central Park, I must have gotten on the wrong trail, for a policeman came running toward me saying, "Get off that trail. That is for saddle horses and you might get run down." I talked a bit smart to him too and he responded that he'd go crazy if he couldn't scold someone occasionally. Both policemen were Irish.

I came a different route back to the West Coast. The beauty of the timber in Pennsylvania was impressive. In William County, Ohio, I stopped to visit cousins. My father had been born there, so it was of great interest to me. Before, it had only been a name on a map. When I left, my aunt put a quart of apple butter in my suitcase and by the time I arrived at another cousin's in Iowa, the jar was broken and the contents spilled over my clothes.

While in Iowa, a neighbor of my relatives heard a noise in his chicken house one night. He got up in his long underwear which had the flap open in back and went out to investigate. He took his gun and his hound. He was slipping along and just as he got to the chicken house door, the hound stuck his cold nose against the man's bottom. He was so startled his gun went off and killed five of his chickens.

In Nebraska, I stopped to visit my sister Ida who, at the time, lived in Elwood where her husband was county clerk. The thermometer had been above one hundred degrees for more than two months. I kept thinking that when I got to the Coast it would be cooler, but I went by way of Los Angeles as I had some friends there. L.A. was the most dreary place of the whole trip, at one hundred and seven degrees in the shade. The weather was hot and everything was inches deep in dust. It seemed like desert two feet from any irrigation canal. There were dried-up riverbeds and desolate heat. I still wonder at the way the population has grown in Southern California, with no cool and balmy air like that in the Willamette Valley.

When I returned home, Buster gave me the brush-off. He acted that way for five months until one warm day in February when my door was ajar and I was lying on the couch. In he came like a great whirlwind. He jumped on me with muddy feet, then rolled on the floor, whined, and groveled. He told me he was all over his pout and wanted to stay at home. Of course, he did from then on.

Buster had been a wonderful watchdog. He never barked at people, but occasionally took hold of a pantleg as a warning. I remember once in Idaho when we saw a tramp coming we wondered what to do, but before the man got near the house Buster went out and lay at the gate and the tramp went right on by. Another time in the country, Nellie and the minister's daughter were alone in the house when in walked a tramp. Buster was in the kitchen, but must have caught his scent; he got up and walked through the dining room into the front room, all ninety-five pounds of him. Mr. Tramp took one look and backed right out through the front door.

The years were catching up with Buster and he took to sleeping a lot. He dug up my fern beds in the shade of the house for a cool spot to lie in. At last, I let the marshal take him to his house where there was plenty of shade and Buster lived out the rest of his life in quiet comfort under a giant oak tree.

The Salem Years

This chapter covers the mature years of Mary's practice after she left Lebanon. Salem was her final home. Here she went through World War I, the Great Depression, and World War II. Her practice broadened to care for patients who had scattered across northwestern and northcentral Oregon.

It was always in my mind that when Nellie was ready for college I would move to a college town. I could make a living anywhere. One day in 1916 a doctor came and made an attractive offer to buy me out. I thought that maybe no one would be there to buy me out when she was ready for college, so I accepted the offer. I liked both Salem and Eugene, but settled on Salem because of the state institutions, canneries, paper mill, and Willamette University.

In Salem, I rented a large house some distance from the business district, thinking I could build a practice from there. I had always lived with my office to make a home for my daughter. I was finally forced to rent a small office downtown, however, on the second floor, with no elevator. I was climbing stairs all day long, at home and at work. When a woman goes into a business she must look sharp and not break her health. My practice was increasing, but the arrangement could not last.

I couldn't seem to find a place near enough to the business district where I could combine a home with an office. One afternoon the answer to my prayer came through a patient who came for an examination. In our visit I told her of my problem. She was the mother of two children and understood all I told her. She went away and soon came back to tell me that she and her husband owned a building in the next block that had two apartments upstairs. One was to be vacated. It would be ideal for me and if I took it her husband would fix it up to suit me. My residence there lasted almost thirty-six years.

Nellie was home alone the first time the landlord, Mr. Moore, came to our apartment after we moved. When I arrived Nellie said, "Mother, Mr. Moore was here and talked a blue streak and never said a word." I always called him "The Warm South Wind."

Whenever the Moores were sick I attended them. Mr. Moore once had an occluded oil gland above his shoulder blade and sometimes it formed an abscess. He was a bit old-fashioned and when the abscess began to swell, he had his wife bind pork fat on it until it burst and drained. The first time he came to me as a patient, the abscess was the size of an egg and he had a piece of pork fat bound to his shoulder. I told him I would have to dissect away the sac before it would stay well. Once I did it he had no more trouble, but he always claimed that I owed him for a pound of pork fat.

In those years I often had to do minor surgery, but every medical doctor needs a reliable surgeon who can routinely perform more difficult operations. Mine was

Dr. Fred Thompson, chief surgeon for the state accident commission. He was personable and had a rapid and accurate technique which meant very little loss of blood. I have never been sorry for my choice. He was always helpful and gave me good advice through the years. I have always depended on other doctors for reliable knowledge and friendship.

I assisted Dr. Thompson who performed two Caesarean operations for one of the Moores' daughters. He delivered the first baby by instrument although it died after several hours. Of the second and third babies—delivered by Caesarean section—one lived and the other died after thirty hours. The child who lived grew up and will soon graduate from a university. Another daughter, the youngest, and her husband died in an auto accident, leaving a ten-month-old boy. The sister adopted him. I attended the daughters' weddings and was present when Mr. Moore died of a *coronary thrombosis* (a broken heart). They always showed appreciation for the care I gave their family.

I have been fortunate over the years to have had such worthy friends as the Moores and Dr. Thompson for whom my respect and understanding have increased. How blessed is a man who finds a friend.

Family medicine was the core of Mary's practice. Like many physicians of the time she played the role of counselor to every patient. The wives spoke of their husbands. The husbands of their wives. And the mothers of their children who needed care. In speeches to local women's organizations she often gave practical advice about family medical care. The following excerpt is from a speech she delivered at a

*local women's luncheon in Oregon: "[Regarding]
'The Proper Training of Children,' it would seem to
be quite as necessary to keep the child's physical
body in the very best condition in order that it . . .
grow naturally. I have nearly always noticed that [in]
the child—be it infant or grown—who is peevish or
irritable, there [is] some physical cause at the bottom
of it. It may be bad digestion, improper action of the
bowels or kidneys; in fact, there will be some part of
the physical body which is not performing its intended functions properly. Every mother wants her
children to be happy and no child is happy unless the
body is well. . . . I am going to give you . . . my ideas
as to some of the conditions for keeping children
healthy. Please consider them and if you do not
believe as I do, at least do not think me a 'crank.'
(1) The location of the house should be on as high
ground as possible . . . well-drained and . . . as much
exposure to the sun as possible—at least twenty-five
feet of space on the east, south, and west. There
should be plenty of sunny windows to let God's
blessed sun in. . . . (2) I have observed that growing
children who sleep with adults do not grow up to
have as much virility or vitality as those who sleep
alone. Such children are usually pale and hollow-
chested. (3) Kids should not have feathers. The mattress may be hair or 'corn husks.' I prefer the latter.
Two sheets with woolen blanket and a sufficient
amount of covers . . . perhaps a little extra over the
feet. (4) Children should wear the combination gowns
with feet in them for . . . a very frequent way for them
to catch cold . . . [is] kicking off the covers at night
during sleep. (5) The sleeping room should be cool*

*with plenty of fresh air. Now some mothers might
think if the room is aired well during the day that it
would be unnecessary to have a window open at
night, but, mothers, your children will never die from
too much fresh air! There should not be a draft blowing over the bed and a screen can be placed between
the open window and bed. (6) There should be sufficient heat in the room before going to bed to dry up
any moisture from the bedding which may have collected from the atmosphere. (7) Children under
twelve years should go to bed at 8 p.m. and get up at
6:00 or 7 a.m. if we wish them to have a quiet,
steady, enduring nervous system. "*

When I came to Salem in 1916, the roads in Oregon
were almost impassable in the winter time. I had not
been in town long before a man came for me to go out
into the country seven or eight miles to confine his
wife. He took me in an old Model T Ford and every
time he came to a mud puddle he stopped, got out, and
took off the chains. He repeated the stopping several
times on the way there. They lived in an old prune drier
in the middle of a plum orchard. I had to wade in mud
to my shoe tops to get into their dwelling where they
had hung quilts, rag rugs, and whatever else they could
to petition off living quarters.

There was only one room for living, cooking, and
sleeping. Nothing looked clean. I had never seen the
woman before and she had had no prenatal care. Thirty
minutes after the baby was born, she went into convulsions. I gave her two hypodermics, one of morphine to
control the convulsions and one of pilocarpine to open
the pores of the skin. Then I wrapped her in a blanket

wrung out of hot water. We had two water bottles and I placed those in the bed with her to keep her sweating. Then I gave her Epsom salts every thirty minutes. I kept her so until the kidneys began to function. I do not know if it could have been done any better in a hospital, but she made a recovery. I hardly hoped that she could.

On a case south of Salem, I drove my car within half a mile of the house, but from there the mud was so deep I knew my car wouldn't make it. While I contemplated how to get across with my two heavy grips, I saw a woman at the house hitching a horse to a buggy. I waited. When she came to the place where I was, I objected to getting into such a rickety old buggy thinking it would fall to pieces or the harness wouldn't hold together long enough for us to get across to the house. However, she assured me that she drove the outfit all the time. This was to be her fifth or sixth child and she was in labor. I got into the buggy with great misgiving.

When we were about a block from her house, we had to cross a bridge over Pringle Creek. Right there the horse began to buck. We were part of the time up on two wheels. The old nag caved around until it broke enough of the harness to get free from the buggy and off it went toward the barn. We walked from there.

Later in the day the baby boy was born. I stayed with her some hours as I didn't think it safe to leave her alone. Her husband came home toward evening and I said to him, "I never was so astonished in my life when I saw your wife in labor, hitching up that horse and coming across the way for me." I thought it would embarrass him, but he slapped his knee and said, "She is the most enduring woman you ever seen." He seemed so proud of her that she could take such good care of herself. The baby grew up and was in World War II as a captain. He had much of his mother in him.

I went into the Lake Labish district to confine a Japanese woman. She was in a very small room with one window about eighteen inches square, two beds, and a trunk. The woman in labor was in one bed and her two little girls in the other. The woman's mother assisted me.

Every so often the grandmother scolded the two little girls for peeking. They covered their heads, but soon I saw two pairs of black, beady eyes peeking out again. I think they witnessed the entire birth. Neither of the girls could have been more than seven or eight.

The U.S. government gathered many Japanese-American families from the Lake Labish district during World War II and placed them in internment camps. Many lost their land, never to regain it.

A Korean man whose wife I confined paid me from his hat. He came to town to pay his bill with a hat full of silver dollars and counted out what he owed me, one by one. The family later went back to Korea and I have often wondered what became of them.

Mary's ledgers indicate that she accepted as payment for her medical services not only checks, cash, and silver, but also horses, cows, furniture, and potatoes. Bartered labor was also common. One invoice, for example, indicates partial payment in the form of "wood sawing."

One day a young girl who had missed her periods came to me for consultation. They will never confess voluntarily so I have a trick statement, "If you have not been with a man, everything will adjust itself. You do not need to worry." Of course, there was denial. I sent her away, but in ten days she was back, asking for an examination. I did not need to ask an embarrassing question. I knew. When I told her she was pregnant, she said she would jump in the river. I said, "Oh, no, you have made a mistake, but you must not add a crime to it. You must tell your mother." She said her mother would turn her out of doors and then I told her that, no doubt, her mother would feel badly, but that she was her friend always and should know about this. Then I told her that if she would like me to tell her mother I would, but it would be much better for her to do it.

She went home and in a few days her mother came to see me. The mother said that her married daughter had no children and wanted one and that she and her husband would take the girl across the state to where the daughter lived on a farm. Her husband planned a leave of absence to go there with her until the baby was born and adopted. She asked if I would come across the state to attend the birth. I said I would if possible. As it turned out, there wasn't time for me to go the two hundred miles, so they had a local doctor attend the girl.

Two years later the mother of the girl came to me extremely perturbed, saying she had found out who the father was. I said, "You do not need to tell me as I have guessed it. No man would drop his business and go to another part of the state for so long unless he was personally interested." The girl's mother was distressed because she didn't know what effect the knowledge would have on the married daughter who had adopted the baby. I said, "Now what purpose would it serve if you told her? Just let that rest. The baby has a good home and is loved and cared for. Why disturb it as it is?" The girl behaved herself and afterwards married a good man, after she told him what had happened. She raised a fine family that she could own before the world.

The implication here seems to be that the girl was naughty and not just a victim, which may represent a social bias of the times. In any case, Mary appears to have assumed that the girl had a certain degree of volitive control over her situation.

The druggist downstairs from my office patronized me and often called me to look after his wife. One day when I came in from Chemawa Indian School I met her at the foot of my stairway. She said that they had been trying to get me all morning. Her husband was ill and they had finally gotten another doctor, but she wished me to see what I could do. The other doctor said he was bilious and ordered calomel.

When I looked him over I noticed that one eyelid drooped and that the pupil of that eye was dilated. He asked me, "What the devil is the matter with my eye?" I asked him how long it had been that way. He said he had noticed it the previous day. I didn't tell him much, but went immediately to my office and called the doctor who had seen him in the morning. I told him that the druggist had some kind of brain trouble and that we should get Dr. Griffith from the state hospital in consultation.

Dr. Griffith thought the trouble was a tumor of the brain. We called a nerve specialist from Portland the next day who suggested it was a low grade of sleeping sickness, that he would get well, but it would be a drawn-out case. I disagreed, for in the two days since I had first seen him he was already inert and they had to move him like a sack of meal. I said, "He is going to die." People never want the doctor who gives them bad news. Thirty-six hours later he died. At the autopsy, they discovered a brain tumor that might have been removed if diagnosed sooner. We found out later that for several months he was troubled with loss of memory, but he and his wife hadn't said anything about it, thinking it unimportant. He was not very old.

Mr. Bellicose was a very small man. I suppose he weighed about one hundred and twenty pounds. What he lacked in size he made up for in energy. He had been a Civil War veteran and just to mention the Civil War was enough to start him fighting it all over again. He was full of pepper.

His first wife died and he remarried a sixty-three-year-old maiden lady. Mr. Bellicose came to me complaining that he had been unable to consummate the marriage. He asked if I could perform an operation on his wife to make it possible. "Otherwise," he said, "I shall have to divorce her as I am just like a young buck." He was then sixty-eight years old. I told him I would see what I could do. One Sunday morning I went to their house and with a local anesthetic passed a speculum, thinking that would help. Mr. Bellicose didn't mention it again, but after two years when he was in my office for something else, I asked him if the little operation I had done on his wife was a success. He slapped his knee and said, "You know, something funny about that operation. After you performed it, I never had any more desire."

Mr. Bellicose lived to be seventy-eight years old. A few weeks before he died I said to him, "Your wife has been a wonderful housekeeper, a good cook, and has taken good care of you." But he complained, "Yes, but she's not a woman anymore."

The Salem school board paid me thirty-five dollars a month to be the school doctor. It was not much, but I made important contacts that way. I also examined girls for the gym and the swimming pool at the Y.W.C.A.

At the close of World War I, the National Y.W.C.A. had some funds left over and decided to have all their physicians and physical directors go to New York for a refresher course. The invitation went out to all the directors and physicians for the Y and because of my work with the girls I received an invitation. I had examined over one hundred and fifty girls for fifty cents each.

In the month before I left for New York in 1919, the Y sent a woman to Salem to organize a business and professional women's club. They elected me president, but I went to New York the next month and they had no meetings. When I came back in January, the flu was raging and all public meetings were forbidden.

In the spring I received the resignation of all the other officers. I took time out from my work to persuade them to hold on until fall when we could start in again. Working women in Salem had never organized before and most were unsure of what it meant. They consented to wait. In the fall they met in my apartment and I made up interesting programs. It was up to me to serve until the club took root, but soon they wanted another woman for president and elected one who showed no interest whatever and never attended a meeting.

About this time I went up to see the state librarian, Cornelia Marvin, who had come to Oregon from a midwestern state and organized the state library. I found her a wonderful person, well-informed, well-educated, and full of enthusiasm and understanding. She agreed to join the club if it left the sponsorship of the Y.

We left the Y and she became chairman of the program committee. Such programs she put on! She kept everybody busy. She found a place to meet in the basement of the Unitarian Church where we sponsored dinners and plays for the girls. Very soon there were over a hundred members. The club is still flourishing after thirty-five years.

Mary loved parties and club gatherings, especially for women. The following is a quote from a newspaper social clip from her Lebanon years: "About thirty of Dr. Mary C. Rowland's friends gathered at her home Wednesday evening and gave her a housewarming in honor of her beautiful new home, which the Dr. just moved into on Sherman Street. It was for ladies only, but it is said that all kinds of 'stunts' appropriate for the occasion were indulged in, such as having the Dr. remove the eyes of a potato with a stove hook, and some of the schoolmarms fed each other cracker crumbs while blindfolded. Elegant refreshments were served and all reported a most enjoyable time even if the men were absent."

It is notable that, in keeping with her patriotic views about supporting the military, she frequently

entertained soldiers on leave during World War II,
providing them with meals in her home.

My second trip to New York was as rewarding as the
first. The doctors who lectured at the Y were women,
and I think maiden ladies, for they all seemed to be at
outs with men doctors. I couldn't help thinking that the
men doctors in the East were different from the ones I
knew in the West or the women had prejudices. Anyway, they seemed like sourpusses.

Mr. Thom, who had been so wonderful to me on my
other trip, seemed to have as much enthusiasm to escort
me around as before. I had an enjoyable time in his
company as well as a very instructive time at different
hospitals. The great Bellevue Hospital was the most impressive of all.

I got along well with a woman physician from
Daytona, Florida, and she expressed the wish that we
might practice together. But then she said, "You would
be at the head of everything and I would just be your
nurse." What a whimsical idea!

I invited a young physical instructor from Alabama to
go with me to see the American Museum of Natural
History. Years later, she came to live in Salem with her
family because I lived here. I lost a good friend when
she died.

After I came back to Salem, Mr. Thom wrote me that
I didn't seem to know what I did to him when I was
there. He wanted me to live back East, but my mind
was not on being tied to anyone. He died a long time
ago now, but he was a very fine man and I enjoyed all
his courtesy to me.

I have never understood women who pretend to hate

men. When I lived in Topeka, a young woman said to me, "I have no use for men." I said, "Then you are no natural woman." She looked at me in great surprise. I do not believe she had ever thought of the natural relationship that exists between men and women. In the language of Longfellow in *The Song of Hiawatha*:

> "As unto the bow the cord is
> So unto the man is woman;
> Though she bends him, she obeys him,
> Though she draws him, yet she follows;
> Useless each without the other!"

I had two very peculiar cases during the years of my practice. A woman who lived at Hood River came down to visit her relatives, and while here she went out on the hills and picked wild strawberries. It was a very warm day. She was of great *avoirdupois*. In the evening she complained of pain in her abdomen. She complained of being very warm but had a normal temperature. I gave her an enema and left orders not to feed her until I came the next day. When I came she was feeling much better. I gave her another enema. She was walking around the room when suddenly she said, "Oh, I'm dying." I was in the kitchen at the time when one of the relatives called me and I went into the room where she was. She had no pulse. Her pupils were dilated and she was covered with perspiration. With the help of the family I got her onto the bed where she sighed once and died. I wanted an autopsy, but her family refused.

There was a couple, the man fifty-seven and the woman forty-seven years of age. They had both been married before and each had been a parent of boys, but no girls. They had one boy together. I never saw them before the woman was in labor. She told me they were poor and wanted to give the baby away when it came, but were afraid of what people would say. She was peculiar in appearance and never looked me in the eye. I told her there were some people who would adopt the baby if she wanted to part with it. There was a neighbor woman there when the baby girl was born. The mother said, "You didn't tell me it was to be a girl." I, of course, laughed and said, "I wanted to surprise you. Do you still want to give it away?"

Her husband had gone to get a practical nurse. She said she would let me know after she talked with him. I went back the next day and everything seemed well. The baby was fine and healthy. The third day the husband called me about four o'clock in the evening and said he believed the baby was dead. I told him he didn't need me, but that he needed the undertaker. However, I went out a couple of hours later to examine the baby, but the undertaker had already taken it away.

The nurse followed me out to the car and said she believed the baby had been accidentally smothered. She was unaware that the mother had expressed an interest in giving the baby away. I hurried off to the undertaker to examine the baby's body, but they had already buried it. Two years later, after the couple had moved to another location, I received a letter from the woman asking me what, in my opinion, had been the cause of her baby's death. I didn't answer the letter for if I had I would have told her what my opinion was.

This was before there was any knowledge of crib deaths. The death may have resulted from Sudden In-

fant Death Syndrome, commonly referred to as "SIDS."

Some couples have more children than they want, while others never have any. A woman came to me once with a queer request. She and her husband didn't have any children and she wanted me to find a baby for them. She intended to go away for a while, then bring an adopted baby home to tell her husband that she had given birth to it. I advised her that it would be against the law to perpetrate such a fraud and if her husband ever found it out it would be grounds for a divorce. I told her I couldn't lend my aid to such a scheme.

One of my patients, a friend, came to me complaining that when she tried to swallow her food, it went up into her nose. She had been a patron of mine for a number of years and I knew this was something serious, for she would not fake anything. However, I was unable to diagnose her case. She went to some doctors in Portland and they told her it was diphtheric paralysis. I couldn't agree with that as she had never had diphtheria. Then I sent her to the state hospital to Dr. Frank Griffith, in whom I had great confidence.

He examined her, then told me that she had bulbar paralysis which has no known cure. The disease lasts from one to seven years and is hopeless. Very soon she was unable to swallow and it became necessary to feed her with a stomach tube. It was a distressing thing to see so fine a person gradually getting more and more involved with her trouble. After some years she contracted the flu and I was there when she died.

* * *

It was something to have lived when all the financial world came tumbling down on the hapless heads of people everywhere: banks failing or closing their doors; stocks and bonds suspending payments of interest; farm products rotting on the ground; people milling about, hungry and cold; a distracted government casting about to devise means of feeding and clothing the distressed, to help those unable to adjust themselves. There were suicides, sickness, and death. What a time to distinguish between reality and illusion.

My banker had always advised me to buy bonds with my savings. He said, "If you do not save it when you have it, you never have it." He said all I would have to do then was to cut coupons twice a year. It looked like a proper recompense for all my industry. Life seemed as easy as that, no bother to collect rent or recover money loaned on real estate. It wasn't for one as bewildered as myself to know a wise investment, but with limited information I tried to avoid those who preyed on credulous widows and kept my savings in dependable channels.

The Depression brought a shattered world and it was up to each to retrieve what was left, by industry and careful savings to look to the future as best one might. I managed to extract, with great difficulty, a small amount of money that I had trickled into a savings and loan association. When I first asked for it, the banker said if I would take a twenty-dollar loss and place it in another fund, I might withdraw amounts as I wished. I did. After one year, I attempted to withdraw the money and the banker said I must give sixty days' notice. After sixty days, the banker said the bank didn't have my money yet. After six more months, there was a vigorous monologue on my part demanding my money, with in-

terest. The banker said the bank would be unable to pay
at the rate for which it had contracted, and that it wasn't
required to pay interest after I asked for the money.

After the twenty-dollar loss on so small an amount I
stated that I did not want any further losses. The banker
said that the bank would probably be able to pay me
in another month. The word "probably" bothered me in
view of the hedging of the past year, so I betook myself
to a lawyer.

Through him I obtained a definite promise to pay in
six weeks. At the end of the time I was forced to wait
in the loan company's office for two hours for the person who handled my account. It was to be compound
interest, but I prepared to be satisfied with a simple interest rate. After this episode, whenever I met the man
who had handled the affair, he always looked like the
dog-stealing sheep that he was.

After receiving the money, I placed it in another bank
for six months. Then I heard a rumor that the bank
wasn't too steady. I had a friend who was director of
the bank. I asked him about it and he informed me that
he knew nothing much about the finances of it. I told
him then that I had put my money there because of him.
I asked him, if the bank closed, would he stand good
for what I had in it? To that he replied, "No, Mam, I
will not." "Then," I said, "I know exactly what I'm going to do." That very day I took my money out of the
bank and put it into postal savings. The stocks and
bonds that I had accumulated through the years fell to
almost nothing in value and ceased to pay interest at all.

Those hard years saw many schemes hatched to take
advantage of people's hopes and good will. One doctor
told me that he could paper a room with bogus stocks

which enterprising racketeers had sold him. Some men once involved the superintendent of our schools in a get-rich-quick scheme and he allowed them to use the high school building to promote their stock. It sounded like a dream from heaven but involved government timberland in exchange for a down payment. Unfortunately, many teachers invested and lost their money, and the superintendent of schools lost his job over it. Most people still think he really believed it was a good idea.

A man and woman once came to Salem selling acreage located on an island off the coast of Mexico. The cost: a reasonable down payment and a secured note. They said one could raise anything on the island and that buyers didn't need to be Mexican citizens to obtain title. They made quite a bit of money from merchants, lawyers, and just ordinary people. Some of the buyers even sold their businesses and went to Mexico to find their island, Palmetto del Verde. They discovered that no place on the island was more than two feet above sea level. And while productive, natives had to be hired to keep the blackbirds and ants off the crops. In the end, there was no ready market for the produce.

One victim of the scheme said that the man who promoted the enterprise was headquartered in Los Angeles and that she had gone to his office and collected evidence. The evidence showed that the couple had sold the land several times over. The government subpoenaed the victims and the two promoters were indicted, but the evidence was inadvertently turned over to a confidence trickster working for the promoters. He claimed he was a government agent. The disappearance of evidence forced the government to drop the case.

* * *

A prominent young woman in trouble and desperate once came to consult me about her condition, and I told her I would have to tell her mother. Then, if she wanted me to, I would take her to a rescue home in Portland where she could stay until her baby came. I never asked who the father was, which would have been pointless as she wouldn't have told me. Her mother was anxious for me to take her to Portland.

At the time, the maiden ladies in charge of the rescue home viewed me in a very unfriendly manner. I had previously taken several girls there and it was their policy to persuade the girls to keep their babies.

The mother came to me after the girl had been there some weeks and said that she worried she couldn't keep her baby. I told the mother to write and tell the girl that I knew a wonderful family who had no children and would be able to care for one. They would be glad to adopt it when it came.

The maiden ladies went up in the air over me negotiating the adoption of a baby, but we made a plan for the mother not to write any more about it, and when she saw the girl to tell her she could give it to these people if she wished.

The baby was born healthy and, when it was time for the girl to leave the hospital, I took my daughter and the girl's mother and went after the girl. I stayed with friends in Portland while the girl's mother and my daughter went to the rescue home for the girl and the baby.

We had prearranged to meet the prospective parents in the city park. After they picked me up again, the girl's mother got on a bus and went home. But we drove to the park to meet the future parents.

I had a lovely little speech made up to say when the girl gave the baby to the other mother. However, when the lady came over to my car and the girl handed the baby to her, we all burst out crying and no one said a single word.

Later the girl met the adoptive family in a lawyer's office in Salem and signed the papers that made it official. I have no doubt that the baby grew up loved and without reproach.

Meanwhile, the Portland rescue home women came to Salem to investigate me. They went first to the girl's mother and she told them the girl had done it herself. Then they went to our police matron and she told them she would investigate. She came to see me and we had a long talk.

I told her one could never make me believe it would be better for the girl to drag a little illegitimate baby around and try to make a living for it than to have it in a home where it would be less impaired. The police matron said, "Doctor Rowland, your ideas are exactly the same as mine." Of course, I was not in the business of selling babies. I am sure I did the baby a good turn and the girl too, for afterwards she married a fine man after informing him of the circumstances. The police matron reported back to Portland that she couldn't find anything improper since the girl had made the transfer herself.

I was called to take care of a confinement case near Scio, Oregon, some twenty-eight miles from Salem. I was there all day until five in the afternoon when a baby was born. Twenty-five minutes later another one was born and then, within five minutes, another one popped out. We were all excited. They were premature and I wanted to bring them into the hospital so that I might try to save them, but the parents refused and they all died.

The parents proved to be deadbeats for I was never remunerated for all my work and for the trips I made to see that the mother was making a proper recovery. Those babies were the only triplets I ever delivered in all the years I practiced. Delivering them for free was a forced charity on my part, but I have given much of my service to worthy people.

Once I took care of a broken arm for a woman without payment. Fifteen years later ten dollars came through the mail with a note from the husband saying he had never before had the money to give me.

One day after I had been up all night and had gone to bed in the daytime to rest, a man came to the door. My daughter met him there to tell him I couldn't see anyone that day, but he said it was very important. Finally, I told my daughter to let him come to my bedroom door to tell me what was on his mind. When he looked in he said, "Doctor Rowland, I have a request to make of you. I want you to see that they pass a law against fornication." I said, "You go right home and as soon as I can I will attend to it." Thus we got rid of him. He must have escaped from the state hospital. We never heard of him again.

One day an old gentleman presented himself at my door. He wanted to know if I made examinations for marriage licenses. I answered in the affirmative. He said he represented three old gentlemen, two of whom were seventy-six years and the other seventy-eight. The youngest bride was sixty-four. They planned a triple wedding. He wanted to know if I could give them a wholesale price because of their number.

Everything was arranged to satisfaction, and while he went to get the necessary papers for the records I made a house call. When I returned, my waiting room was full of brides and grooms chattering like magpies.

One talkative old gentleman came into my inner office and began, "The little woman out there whom I am going to marry, I married her once before and we lived together twenty-two years. Then she complained of dizzy spells and wanted to go back East. I didn't want to go, for I had come to this country for my health. Here I am as healthy as an ox. People separated us and she was in the East twenty-two years.

"She came back last fall. I had no money to get married. You understand, I had money but it wasn't where I could get at it. I went to see a judge about it and he said to me, 'Good God, man, there are thousands of couples living together who never had a ceremony said over them. Go, and live with her until you get the money and then marry her.' That is what I have done. We have lived together six months; now I have the money and today we are going to marry. And Dr. Rowland, I want to recommend to you the Lord Jesus Christ for he has been everything to me."

There were to be no decorations, which seemed a pity to me, so I gave each one a daffodil. The evening paper said, "They were to be married somewhere in Salem, a triple wedding. Their combined ages were four hundred and thirty-one years, with an eligibility of twelve hundred dollars a month ... [under] the Townsend Plan." It added that the decorations were daffodils.

This was truly a springtime activity in the autumn of life.

A pathbreaking proposal that led to the Social Security Act of 1935, the Townsend Plan had proposed a two hundred dollar per person monthly payment for citizens sixty years or older.

There had been no word of Uncle Henry for eighteen years. One day in our apartment in Salem, Nellie was standing at the window looking out when suddenly she exclaimed, "Mother, across the street is a man who looks like Uncle Henry." Sure enough, there he stood on the corner begging nickels from passersby. He seemed to be doing a thriving business judging from the rattle of coins and the smile on his face. But again he disappeared.

Six months later I met him face to face. He looked at me and said, "Why, Doctor Rowland!" After eighteen years! I brought him home with me and asked him where he had been all those years. Well, he said he had been in California part of the time. He was never very definite, saying things like "up and down the coast," "up and down the highways," "never far from the ocean," "riding when invited," "walking when necessary."

When the weather was mild, he slept under a tree near the river in which he washed his clothes and bathed. "The water feels good," he said. His clothing smelled like fresh laundry that had hung in the sunshine all day. His faded blue overalls had been laundered many times.

Overjoyed to meet someone he had known, he talked

of many things. At times his mind wandered off into the unreal, but perhaps not more than one might expect from one so old. He was interested, he said, that Russia was trying to do away with the Christian bible. Then I asked him if he had ever been in Russia. "Why, yes, in Harbin [China] and Archangel [Russia]. Do you know what happens in Archangel? Well, the sun goes down and in half an hour it comes up again. Some people think there's only one sun, but I had to go to Archangel to find out about that one up there."

I said, "Uncle Henry, were you ever married?" "No," he said. "When I was young they told me that I would have to earn a wife. I've worked hard all my life, but you wait, I'll turn the world upside down yet before I die." Later, he said something about his daughter and I asked, "Why Uncle Henry, have you a daughter?" He looked at me a bit startled and then his eyes twinkled. He said, "You know, when I am out in the woods by myself, I talk to lots of people." The loneliness of the poor creature! No doubt, the woods were peopled with the loved ones he had never had.

I gave him some money and told him to come back the next day, that he might get some snapshots of himself. It was more than three weeks before we saw him again. He said he had been unable to find the stairway to our apartment. I believed him, for he said he had muttered, "She is the only friend I have on earth and now I have lost her." The cloudiness then passed from his mind and he talked of the people we had known in Lebanon.

In speaking of the minister's wife in whose barn he had lived while there, he said, "She didn't like me. She could have greased me up and swallowed me down! She thought I was a jack rabbit!"

He said it was good to sleep out on the ground when the weather was good, but when it was bad he always had enough money to get a clean bed. He would go into people's gardens, dig a spud, and take an old tin can down by the river to cook it over a little campfire. Very soon he had something good to eat. Life to him was as simple as that; he seemed as happy as a bird and as unfettered. Once he was arrested for begging on the street. The judge asked him what he had to say for himself and he replied, "Well, Judge, it's this way. I'm too old to work and too honest to steal." The judge said, "There's the door, get out of here." He seemed to have no particle of self pity and took great satisfaction that he had been able to get along so well. In my house he was very polite, never trying to take advantage because we were gentle with him.

A night or two before he last came to our apartment he had slept between the road and the river. During the night a skunk had run directly over him. He said, "You bet I didn't hit him, but I yelled at him and he sure dusted himself down the road to take the news to Mary."

And now Uncle Henry is gone again. The years have slipped away. Has he not had as much from life as most of us? His wants, being simple, have all been supplied. He has had his freedom. I have no doubt he is in some comfortable location. Has he found, perhaps, by the side of the road, the answer to life's great quest?

There was a woman in the country who had been trying to persuade me to buy some of her fifteen acres, but the state land board held a mortgage on the property and she was unable to pay interest or taxes. Finally, I bought a half acre and the board told me to pay her no money, but to bring her with me and pay them. I did so and she didn't receive any of the money she badly needed. I therefore rustled up someone else to buy more of her land.

My good friend Lena Belle Tartar had been teaching high school for years and had roomed in various places. I persuaded her to buy an acre next to mine. The woman received some of Lena Belle's payment. I felt that I had done the owner a good turn, as well as myself: to get such a nice neighbor as Lena Belle.

I took money from my postal savings to start a house in Salem and bought handmade shakes from a couple of young men at Mehama. My carpenter, one of the best, needed the work and I paid him four dollars a day. Common labor I got for two dollars a day. It was not much for wages but it helped them and meant a lot to me.

Mary's carpenter was her brother-in-law Perry Ginther, who managed a busy home construction business in his later years.

I didn't have enough money to finish the house right away. And later, before the Depression was over, I garnered enough to build another house on the half acre. It took me ten years to pay all I owed on the second house, which I rent.

My houses were outside the city limits so I had at the time no water. I had a well put down and found an abundance. Eventually, I bought into the city system and advertised my pump for sale for one hundred dollars. A German man from Sheridan bought it.

My renter said he would take the pump out and have it ready for the buyer to pick up. When he tried to take the pump out, he found it to be more of a job than he'd anticipated. The well was one hundred and five feet deep and the pipe was too heavy for two men to lift out. When the German came for the pump, I told him that I had had to get a plumber with three men and equipment to remove it and if he did not want to pay the extra amount, thirty-eight dollars, I would give him his money back. He took the money and went home.

Then I advertised the pump again for one hundred and fifty dollars and sold it for that amount. The pump was as good as new and it had cost me two hundred and fifty dollars.

After the Depression, my heart began acting up so I was unable to take more confinement cases. I received a letter from the state board telling me that I had a remarkable record of never having had a death from infection following a confinement.

I only had one death ever following a confinement. It occurred like this. I never saw the woman until three hours before labor began and she was in a bad way with a kidney involvement. Her husband had been warned during the previous two confinements that she should have no more pregnancies. The baby presented with the breech and I had another doctor on the case with me. The baby was stillborn. The husband had employed a young girl as a nursemaid to care for his wife, and as soon as the baby was born he dismissed me saying that if he needed me he would send for me. Eight days later he sent for me to hurry out to his house. When I arrived, his wife was dying from convulsions. She left a house full of children. I always felt I could have saved her if I had had the chance.

In all my cases I saw to it that everything was as clean as possible. When a baby was born I never left any part of the placenta or membranes to cause an infection. In all the years I practiced there was no careless work. A doctor deals with human life and if he is careless he loses the most precious thing an individual has.

When my granddaughter Carolyn was three months old, my daughter and her husband wanted to go to a New Year's party so they left her with me. We put her basket on the daybed just through the wall from my bed. I got up once or twice to see that she was all right. I intended to keep her until the next day as they were to be home late.

Carolyn, born on September 25, 1937, was the daughter of Nellie and M. T. Madsen Jr. Nellie married "Ted" Madsen on February 23, 1935.

It was difficult for me to sleep with all the horns blowing, car doors closing, and the responsibility of the baby. The last time I looked at the clock it was three o'clock in the morning. After that, I slipped into a doze until I felt the bedcovers go tug, tug, tug. Instantly, all my faculties were as alert as they could possibly be. I thought that I was alone in my apartment with no one but the baby and my canary. I knew it couldn't be either. I thought that maybe it was my imagination when tug, tug, tug went the bedclothes again. By then I was paralyzed with fright. I listened to determine if I could hear anyone breathe, or if there was any movement in the room. I heard nothing. Suddenly tug, tug, then I reached over and turned on the light and I heard and felt something jump off the bed.

After diligent search, the only thing I found was a gnawed apple in the kitchen. I couldn't imagine how a rat could have gotten into my apartment, living upstairs as I did. The rest of the night I spent watching to see that it didn't get at the baby or the bird.

I had rat poison, but it was several years old. I applied some to crackers and placed them in the bedroom and front room.

The next evening, I went to a moving picture show and in the picture the actors were playing with poker chips. That night I dreamed there were poker chips under my head and some of them were up edgeways and hurting my head. Suddenly the pain awakened me and I found the rat chewing on the hair at the back of my head.

Was I scared? Man! It seemed bent on eating me up. Again I pulled the light cord but found that the rat had eaten all the poison off the crackers. The poison was so old it had separated.

There was no more sleep that night. Something more efficacious had to be done. I said, "That fellow is not going to sleep with me another night." You can't trust a rascal.

The next morning about ten o'clock, as I was sitting in my living room, Mr. Rat came out of the kitchen, walked the full length of the living room—fat and sleek and bold as brass—and went out into the waiting room. That afternoon I set a trap in a place where it was impossible for the rat to get at an apple placed behind it without passing directly over the trap. That evening about seven-thirty I heard a little rustling in the kitchen. I thought, "Go ahead, little boy. Help yourself. Get all the apple you want." Rustle, rustle. Suddenly, *wang* went the trap, then such a bumping and thumping and squealing as one ever heard.

I called the owner of the trap to come right away before Mr. Rat could get away. He certainly made a quick trip and came booming up the stairway to finish off the invader. We did not, at the time, know how the rat got into the apartment, but we knew how he went out, wrapped in a newspaper. It was a very popular funeral.

Later we found a small hole around the plumbing under the kitchen sink where he had made his entrance from the basement. I put a piece of tin over the opening and we have had no visitors of his stripe since.

When my granddaughter Carolyn was fifteen months old, it was necessary for my daughter to go into the business world. I therefore brought up Carolyn, a big undertaking for one as old as I was at the time, but I did the best I could and she is a fine person now in high school, sixteen years old and a great comfort to me.

Mary encouraged her daughter Nellie to obtain an education and become a businesswoman. After she was married and running a small retail business in Salem, Mary took on the role of raising Nellie's daughter Carolyn. Mary's career at the time was winding down—only a few friends were accepted as patients—and she relished the opportunity to have her granddaughter with her constantly. Nellie lived nearby and saw Carolyn regularly, but in 1939 Mary took on the primary role of raising her granddaughter.

Physician at Chemawa

This chapter presents incidents that occurred while Mary was staff physician at the Chemawa Indian School, an appointment she held while living in Salem. The Chemawa chapter is not intended to follow the Salem chapter chronologically. Nestled in this chapter is also a portrait of a friendship she maintained with a Siwash Indian woman.

The Indian school where I worked near Salem was first established in 1880 at Forest Grove. It was moved to Chemawa (sha-maw-wa) about 1885. The U.S. government owns roughly four hundred and thirty-six acres of land there, some in the rich Lake Labish bottomland with its soil nearly twenty feet deep. The Southern Pacific Railroad passes directly through the middle of the collection of Chemawa school buildings and, despite trains passing through at all hours of the day and night, there has never been an Indian child killed by a train.

In 1918, Dr. Frank Brown, an eye, ear, nose, and throat specialist in Salem, recommended me for the position of physician to the Indian school. I first went to the school—six miles north of Salem—to see about the job, but Superintendent Harwood Hall was not at home.

His wife, however, was eager to talk with me. I never thought that she might have any influence in the matter, so after my interview I left with a feeling of frustration that Mr. Hall was not there himself. That evening, however, he called me at home and said that I had been hired.

Mrs. Frances Hall soon became one of my most valued friends. Mr. Hall was a fine and decisive executive, though I did not always agree with him on every matter.

As my contract stipulated twice-weekly visits to the school, I thought it would be easy for me to go there regularly yet carry on my practice in town. I held the position for nine years and grew very interested in the history of the Indians, particularly in the Northwest. I made a list of all the tribes that Lewis and Clark mentioned on their trip. I read many histories such as Agnes Laut's *'Adventures of England' on Hudson Bay*; the reports of Lewis and Clark, Captain Bonneville, and Jedediah Smith; and Washington Irving's *Astoria or, Anecdotes of an Enterprise Beyond the Rocky Mountains*.

Before the appointment to the Indian school, I knew very little about the tribes of Indians or what Indians were really like. I found it interesting that most of the early trappers had Indian wives. A few years after the Lewis and Clark trip, many of the Columbia Indian tribes completely disappeared, destroyed largely by measles. Mr. Hall informed me that whenever we had a disease at the school that affected the lungs we were sure to lose some of the Indians. While serving at Chemawa, I only had three cases of measles because I isolated them as soon as they were diagnosed. All recovered.

The doctor whom I replaced at Chemawa afterwards became the county doctor. He must have resented me for having the position for he told a Salem newspaper that there was an epidemic of measles at Chemawa and no quarantine. He added that he had no authority to do anything about it because it was on U.S. government property. I talked with the superintendent about the article and we decided to make a statement to the same newspaper that we had had three cases three weeks previously and had isolated them. We also said that the patients were recovering or convalescent. (Incidentally, the doctor who caused us this distress later died of something he shouldn't have had.)

It was the custom to examine all the children when they arrived from home for school to see that they had no contagious diseases. One morning a group of little girls came to the hospital for their routine examinations. They didn't seem more than six years old and wouldn't answer any of my questions. Although Indian children often pretend to be mute with strangers, I wasn't certain that they understood my English. Finally I said, "To what tribe do you belong?" One of the little girls looked at me, then dropped her eyes to the floor and said, "We all Crow."

It is characteristic of the Indian not to tell all he knows nor give confidence until he feels sure he is talking to a friend. I am somewhat that way myself. If a person is kind to me and invites my confidence I am likely to bloom and tell much.

I had hardly started working at Chemawa when flu struck the school. A doctor came down from Browning, Montana, with a group of teenage boys and one of them was ill when he arrived. I asked the Montana doctor to come to the hospital and have a look at the boy. He was quite rough toward the boy and said he didn't think he was as sick as he let on. The boy seemed almost unconscious to me and his skin had a bluish cast. It was our first case of the flu, the first of five hundred and thirty-six cases.

In a few days we had many cases. Mr. Hall wanted me to announce in the paper that it was a very mild outbreak, but I said, "I think it would be very unwise because some of the children will die." Mr. Hall said, "You do not think they are sick enough to die!" I said, "Yes, I certainly do."

The boy from Montana died the next morning. We lost two the next day and Mr. Hall was soon declaring that it was the plague. He worried all the time for fear that I would quit and he would be unable to get another physician. At first I was afraid of the epidemic, but I said to myself, "I might just as well die of the disease as be scared to death."

Our Protestant instructor at the school did quit and told me that when I thought it was safe she would return. The Catholic priest, old Father Goll, never missed a day. His mere presence gave the children comfort. My presence also gave them comfort. The hospital had fifty beds, but the dormitories were full too.

I managed the sick by going to the school at seven o'clock in the morning, visiting the dormitories, then selecting the worst cases for the hospital. We soon had one hundred children there and put up screens to separate them. We hardly had room to walk between the beds. We had one practical nurse from Salem. My head nurse was Mrs. Codding, a Coos Bay Indian who had graduated from Carlisle Indian School in Pennsylvania.

She was a widow and had a little daughter. She was fine with the children and the little girls who were her assistants. It was a sad time for the children's parents, no doubt, as we lost nineteen children. As people were dying all over the world from diseases I do not believe our death rate was above average.

It has been estimated that more than 500,000 Americans died in the 1918–19 Spanish influenza epidemic and about twenty million worldwide.

Often the children coughed blood onto the screens. One little girl, Della Moss from Montana, was very ill and was coughing constantly in spite of all we could do. One morning when I went into the room where she was with dozens of others, I noticed that she was puffed out like a toad. At first I was afraid to touch her. Then I put my hand on her and discovered that she had coughed so hard that she had ruptured an air fessicle. This forced air into her tissues. She was a pitiful looking sight. A day or two later Father Goll asked how I thought Della was and I said I thought she was a little better. He said, "Excuse me, Dr. Rowland, but I don't believe she can live."

Mrs. Codding had earlier sent an urgent message to Mr. Hall saying: "Della Moss is passing away, can you get word to Father Goll."

I said, "Well, she may not, but she seemed a little better this morning." I had noticed something that the good Father had not. When I came into the room little Della's eyes were on the door looking for me. When a person is about to die they are indifferent to everything. She recovered.

During the epidemic we had three cases of meningitis. Two of the children with meningitis died. The one who recovered was uncoordinated and walked as if she were drunk. She died later of something else.

The flu started in the Indian school in September and raged for nearly four months, then began to subside. My daughter and I both had it at once as did our friend Lena Belle who lived in a studio half a block from my apartment. Her father, a professor at Oregon State College at Corvallis, came to take care of her. I loaned him bedding and he bought a cot to sleep on until she began to recover. Nellie and I had no one to care for us and Nellie seemed very allergic to the flu. Her kidneys failed to act for thirty-six hours. It was impossible to get nurses or help because everyone was ill and when a person died there was no one to attend the funeral.

I was hardly able to wait on Nellie but did as well as I could. Another doctor called on us and prescribed soda pop. She drank one hundred and forty-four bottles in all and I think the fluid was a great help to her. When Lena Belle began to improve, her father went back to Corvallis to teach and her mother came to care for her. Her mother said she didn't like to eat at restaurants and offered to cook for all of us if I would let her use my stove. She was sent from heaven. Her sense of humor, funny sayings, and pleasant base voice were lifesaving for Nellie and me. We had been shut in so long without any care at all.

One day she told of a couple who had plenty of money but continued to live meagerly in an out-of-the-way place. "They could've been just as happy in a tin can," she said.

The flu finally passed, leaving thousands of new graves. At one time they said the baggage room at the railway station was piled to the ceiling with caskets of the dead waiting to be shipped to places of burial. I lost a young teacher in Salem, a beautiful person in the full bloom of young womanhood. Her mother and sister had taken care of her, but she only lasted three days. I'll never forget that mother, how efficient she was, and how well she held up as she watched her beloved daughter slip away.

Doctors worked day and night. I don't know what present doctors will do if there is another serious epidemic. Today doctors refuse to go to patients in their homes, but make them come to their offices or a hospital before examination.

Some of our Indian boys fought in the First World War. I recall one boy, on whom I performed a tonsillectomy, had been in France during the war. Indians are very quiet unless something loosens their inhibitions. After his tonsils were removed and he was coming out from the anesthetic he grew loquacious and said, "In France some people said they'd like to see an American Indian, and I said, 'Right here is one of them.' " He tossed his head as he said this and I knew he was proud of his ancestry. American Indians have distinguished themselves in many fields. It is said that an Indian led the planes that stopped the Japanese at Midway during World War II. Senator Charles Curtis who became Vice President was an Indian.

A couple of years ago I picked up three hitchhiking Indian boys north of Salem. After they got into my car and we were going along, one of the boys suddenly said, "Some folks don't like Indians." I said, "Some folks don't like anyone but themselves." Pretty soon he remarked, "I'm Jim Thorpe's boy; you know who Jim Thorpe was? Well he was the all-American athlete." I informed him that I knew who he was.

Mr. Hall used to say that the solution to the Indian question was that they would melt into the white race. I know this is taking place all the time, but it surprised me that during my tenure at the school many of the Indian students were already more white than Indian. Many had barely enough Indian blood to qualify for entrance. Personally, I've known many people who claim Indian blood.

Some years after the influenza epidemic, Mr. Hall called me and said there was an unconscious boy at the Deaconess Hospital in Salem who had been hit by a truck. Mr. Hall asked me if I would go and see if it might be one of our children. The boy had been there for three days and they told me he had not moved since being brought in. Neither had he taken nourishment.

When I went into the ward the nurses were all clustered around his bed. I examined him, then told the nurses that I would have an ambulance take him to Chemawa. They objected to moving him, saying that it would surely kill him. I said, "Oh, no it will not." In examining him, I had noticed that when he heard my voice his eyelids fluttered. That wouldn't have been the case if he were really unconscious. As soon as we got him to the hospital at Chemawa he asked for a glass of milk. I asked him why he had played dead with all those nurses hovering about him. He didn't answer me for a minute, but then said, "Too many women."

One day I was called to Chemawa at about four o'clock in the morning and arrived to find a boy on the ground. He was a fourteen-year-old Klamath Indian who had fallen out of a second-story window. His parents had known that he walked in his sleep, but had not reported the fact to the superintendent when he entered the school. He was subsequently put in a second-floor dormitory. He had walked in his sleep, climbed out the window, and fallen to the ground. When I arrived, some of the employees and the superintendent were standing near him as he lay on the ground, but on examination I discovered that he had broken his neck and was quite dead.

There is a false belief that people who walk in their sleep never receive injuries. Sometimes they do walk in dangerous places and receive no harm, but known sleepwalkers should always sleep on the first floor. Often the sleepwalker has no memory of doing anything out of the ordinary, just as the epileptic performs acts of which he has no recollection. In the light form of epilepsy called *petit mal*, the patient does not lose consciousness altogether, but may sometimes perform acts of great violence without any later memory of what has transpired. Sometimes they steal without realizing why. In such cases, it is hard to convince the public that the act was not deliberate. Of course, these persons at times are a menace to society.

Mary's understanding of petit mal *epilepsy was a misconception. In the mild* petit mal *form the patient is quite unconscious but does not undergo seizures. In the* grand mal *form of epilepsy the patient is unconscious and undergoes seizures. The kleptomaniac,*

one with an abnormally persistent impulse or ten-
dency to steal, may have sometimes been mistaken in
Mary's day for a mildly afflicted epileptic because of
the accompanying amnesia.

During World War I, we paid thirty-one dollars per hundred weight for sugar. At the restaurants they served it
in little squares done up in paper. Ichthyol, a fossilized
fish oil from the Tyrol Mountains, was thirty-two dollars a pound. It was a medicine that I used much of in
my work at Chemawa and it happened that we had several pounds of it. A druggist in Salem found out that we
had some and went to the school and told the superintendent that I had said he could buy a pound at the price
we had paid. I told the superintendent that we had no
right to sell government property and that I needed it
for our children. He then made the druggist bring it
back. I don't know if it was right or not for me to have
made a fuss about it.

The employees at Chemawa were, for the most part,
honest and conscientious, and were doing four times as
much work as the U.S. government was paying them
for. I was contracted to call there twice a week, but
went every day as there was always someone ill. It was
very enjoyable work as I liked to associate with the
other employees.

One couple employed there, however, had problems.
I knew neither of them personally. The woman had
asthma and from the reports I gathered her husband was
not very sympathetic toward her. One night she was
coughing badly and keeping him awake. Finally, she got
out of bed to go downstairs to get a remedy and as she
went her husband remarked that he hoped she would die

with her asthma. She waited downstairs until he was
asleep, then took a hatchet upstairs and finished him.
Afterwards, she walked six miles to Salem to the police
station and gave herself up.

She told the police that she had killed her husband.
Neither Mr. Hall nor anyone else there knew anything
about it until the sheriff came and communicated what
the woman had said. Mr. Hall went over with the sheriff
to the house the couple had occupied and found the man
in the bed with blood all over the walls and bed. She
had hacked him terribly. Mr. Hall then remarked, "I
guess she told the truth." So far as I know she is still in
the penitentiary under a life sentence.

There were some other tragic incidents and unusual
cases that occurred while I was at the school. A beautiful girl who had graduated from Chemawa had trained
as a nurse in Portland. She had decided to go back
home to Alaska to visit her people before she went into
permanent work. She made the visit, but on the way
back, somewhere between Alaska and Seattle, she disappeared from the boat on which she had booked passage. No one was ever able to find out what happened
to her.

In another incident, one of our girls was on shipboard
from Alaska to Chemawa when she was raped by two
negro waiters. The girl was fifteen. I treated the girl for
the venereal disease she had contracted. The waiters
were subsequently sent to McNeil Island for life.

The U.S. government sued the ship company for
damages and Mr. Hall stood for the government as
guardian of the girl. When the trial came, the government subpoenaed us to testify in Seattle. On the witness
stand I explained that she had been penetrated and had

a purulent discharge, for which I treated her. The steamship company's lawyer said, "Did you make a test?" I said, "Do you mean a smear or a blood test?" He said, "Well, whatever you have to do." That was the only question he asked me. We got a verdict and the court awarded the government eight thousand dollars on behalf of the girl.

This case was Margarett Sutton vs. Pacific Steamship Co. The assault occurred on the Steamship Admiral Evans. The two men were convicted, sentenced to life, and entered McNeil Island Federal Prison on February 22, 1924. One was paroled after ten years. They both claimed innocence at the trial and there were some irregularities in the testimony. The captain of the ship even used racial slurs during testimony and these were written into the court record. The girl, whose stateroom was next to the waiters' quarters, stuck by her sworn statement and identification of the attackers throughout the trial. The man who received parole was commended by the chief steward during the trial: "As far as being responsible I never had a man on board the ship at any time that was more trustworthy or honest in my opinion and well liked and competent." The other convicted felon was eventually transferred to Leavenworth Prison in Kansas, a higher security facility.

Another time I diagnosed a seventeen-year-old girl from Klamath Falls as having a fibroid. I brought her into the hospital in Salem where one of the doctors looked at her and told me he thought she was pregnant. He said, "Doctor Rowland, when the surgeon gets in there you are going to be so embarrassed." I said, "That might be, I do not pretend to be infallible, but on examination it did not feel like a pregnancy." The morning Dr. Thompson and I operated on her the other doctor stayed at the hospital to see for himself.

The girl had been the subject of much speculation at the school and among her people. It proved to be a fibroid that weighed seventeen pounds. Because of her appearance and the size of the cyst, it was no wonder it had confused everyone. The girl made a fine recovery and was not shunned. Of course, had it turned out to be a pregnancy, she would have been sent home.

Our custodian of property was a little man who was very careful with government property. The girls at the hospital were forever breaking the thermometers and he often refused to give them more. I had to replace them by buying more uptown in Salem. One day when he was making an invoice he came to tell me of something he couldn't find at the hospital but supposed should be there. He said he had looked everywhere and couldn't find it, but that it was listed as property of the school. He suggested I had made away with it.

I asked, "What is it you are hunting for?" He said, "A placenta." I said, "Man, do you know what a placenta is? That is what is commonly called the afterbirth." Was his face red!

I once asked a teacher to make out a list of the Indian names of children who attended school. This is the list: John Wades In Water, Mabel Pretty Snake Woman, Jim Eagle Ribs, Iron Pipe, First One, Shoots First, Wolf Tail, Yellow Wolf, White Dog, Little Dog, White Plume, Little Plume, Weasel Head, Black Eagle, Half Moon, Night Gun, Four Horns, Other Medicine, Takes

A Gun, Bull In Sight, Calf-Looking, Chief Night, Bear
Chief, Wolf Chief, Lone Chief, Bird Rattle, Running
Rabbit, No Runner, Pete Butterfly.

Pete Butterfly tended the furnace. I didn't know just
how it happened, but he fell into red hot coals and
burned his hands and arms up to his elbows. He also
burned his feet and legs to his knees and his face. When
I arrived at the hospital he was in terrible agony and
said, "Oh, I'm going to dead, I'm going to dead." I said
to him, "Now Pete, you listen to me. I'll help you,
you'll see." First I gave him a hypodermic of morphine.

During World War I, a French doctor had used a
combination of paraffin and resins to spread on burns
with a spray. I obtained a product of this type from
Johnson & Johnson and went out daily to put it on Pete.
We melted it over a spirit lamp and rolled it on with a
cotton swab. The paraffin kept the air away and pro-
tected the new skin as it began to form.

Every few days Mr. Hall would ask when I planned
to do the skin grafting, but I never had to do any. The
only scar left was on his instep. The doctors do not use
that treatment at all now as far as I know, but it still
seems to me a wonderful treatment for burns.

In 1923, a friend and I took our daughters and went to
Nye Beach, Oregon, for a two-week vacation. Driving
from Newport to Agate Beach, I picked up a little old
Indian woman who was trudging along by the side of
the road. She seemed to be in her eighties. Life had
been hard for her and she was then a very lonely old
woman. In the fine skin of her face time had woven a
million wrinkles. Her dark eyes were sad and dim.

She said to me, "Me no Indian. Indian white man

name. Me, Siwash. Me old, so old. Me try find out sometime. Now, me no care."

She possessed two very small houses, one at Newport in which she lived, and one on the north slope of Yaquina Head, east of the lighthouse. She rented one when she could for five dollars a month. That pittance was her sole income.

When she was younger, she climbed down by the tide-washed rocks to gather clams, then went out over the hills for wild huckleberries. This was too difficult now and she felt she was lucky to be able to gather a few sticks of wood to cook her simple food.

I told her about the Indian school at Chemawa where I was the physician and she seemed to feel my friendly attitude. During the vacation, I took her back and forth to her little houses, a distance of three or four miles. One day we drove her deep into the timber along the coast and she seemed so at home in the woods that she told us many things about the trees, shrubs, and vines. She pulled some roots from the ground and showed us how she treated them and wove them into baskets. She knew nothing of books, but was very educated, trained in those things she needed to know to live. She had special names in her native tongue for everything around her. She grew to confide in me without restraint.

I asked about the tattoo marks down both sides of her chin and she said, "That nice thing for Siwash maid. When me small child, my mother go deep woods. She gather certain kind roots. She take to hilltop. Find rock with deep place. She take other rock and pound root until juice come out. She rub small maid child till blood come. Then she rub juice in. Three, four, five days, face get big. Me no eat. Long time get well. Me nice Siwash

maid. . . . When me so big, maybe sixteen, long come
white man. Beautiful white man. Me go with him. Me
his woman. By-n-by, come baby boy. That so nice. Everybody happy. He lived to be twelve, then white father
he say, 'Send boy to New York to learn white man
ways.' Long come evil spirit. What you call, measles.
Evil spirit take boy. Boy buried on hilltop above lighthouse still.

"By-n-by, come baby girl. She so nice. She beautiful.
When she so big father send her New York. She stay
white grandfather. He rich man. He proud man. He
teach Siwash maid white man ways. She grow more
beautiful. She come home, once, twice. Then white father, he die. He buried on hilltop above lighthouse. Still
on lighthouse. O me!

"White grandfather not let Siwash maid come see Siwash mother. Daughter marry white man. By-n-by she
get what you call bad cough. Two, three years she die.
Body come. She buried on hilltop above lighthouse. I
take you there. You is tillicum docket." I am told this is
Chinook for great friendly doctor.

And so we climbed one day to the top of the hill
above the lighthouse, near Cape Foulweather on Yaquina Head, overlooking the wide Pacific. There under
the sighing fir trees, she had placed her dead, one by
one. They were all her own now and no white man
could take them from her. She could come and go as
she pleased and commune with them in her own way. It
was the most precious spot in the world to her, despite
the fact that here she saw her star of destiny going
down.

At present there is no beach on the north side of Yaquina Head, though she told me that formerly there had

been a narrow strip of sand. Her little boy had loved to ride his horse on this beach. One evening she saw him riding there, back and forth, when suddenly there was a noise like a thousand thunders, a great rumbling. Then all the beach and part of the mountain slid off into the Pacific. She thought her boy had gone down with it, but directly he came up over the hill on his horse. It must have been a narrow escape.

She told me that her husband had owned the land alongside the little stream that flows across Agate Beach, but after her husband died other white men came and stole it.

There came a day when she invited me into her tiny house at Newport, to see her precious material things. From a pocket in her underskirt, she took a key with which she unlocked an old trunk. "Me not show these all white mans. Me no like. You is tillicum docket."

Tenderly she removed each garment woven with beads like those the Hudson's Bay Company had used to barter with the Northwest Indians. There were ropes of beads, chains of metal and sea shells, and buckskin smocks with fringes tipped with tinkling thimbles. I wondered how many beaver skins her husband had traded for all this finery for his barbarian woman, beautiful and diminutive. What a sensation she must have created as she moved among her sisters with scintillating beads and tinkling thimbles. To her now they represented the precious material things of a vanished world where she had been so happy and content. She told me that the Smithsonian Institute had offered to buy her things but "Me no sell." Years later I met some Silets Indians (this woman was a Silets) and they informed me that Julia Megginson had died. No doubt, they buried her up on Yaquina Head near those she loved. It was a release to her and Death had come as a friend.

When I was appointed to be physician for the Indian school, I had been in Salem only two years and my practice was not yet very extensive. Therefore I was able to give more time to my Indians. As time went on I became acquainted with more people and my practice increased. By the time my daughter was ready for college I had more work than I should have been doing. Not only in Salem was there work, but many of my former patients from Lebanon came to me, as well as many from surrounding areas as far away as the coast.

As I look back now, I was always delivering a baby and I never wished to disappoint the mother by being away when the hour came. I seemed all the time to have been sitting around waiting for someone to have a baby, or else I was busy delivering one. I gave many anesthetics for other doctors and assisted in the operations on my own patients.

In the Indian Service, there was an eye, ear, nose, and throat doctor who traveled from one Indian hospital to another doing his special work. Together we did two hundred and fifty sets of tonsillectomies. He taught me exactly how to remove tonsils and required me to do fifty sets under his supervision. After that I removed many in my Salem office in cases unrelated to Chemawa.

In 1927, I resigned my work at Chemawa and went to Chicago to take a course at DeLee's Lying-in Hospital. While there I attended a number of clinics at the Cook County Hospital. Of course, I also spent some time at the Field Museum and the Chicago Art Institute.

At the time they were building the great Stevens Hotel and it was marvelous to see tiny men fasten hooks onto great blocks of stone and then slowly lift them by machinery to the top of the structure. There a man no bigger than a fly reached out and pulled the stone over to let it settle into place. Physically man is weak, but his mind is the greatest thing in the animal kingdom.

Chicky Boy

My sister May had wanted for a long time to give me a canary because she raised so many. When my activities were finally restricted, I agreed to try one. That was how Chicky Boy came to live in my apartment. He was three weeks old and one could tell he was a male because he kept trying to swell his throat to sing. Canaries do not sing much before they are six months old.

One day I let him out into my big living room to see how he would take to it. He acted frightened out of his wits. He flew up on the drapes, pictures, and mirror, and when he was tired he settled on the floor. We took the bottom away from the cage and set the cage down over him.

He had the freedom of my entire apartment. I kept his food in his cage, but he was usually sleeping in the window drapes or on the plate rail in the dining room.

One night I came home about midnight and when I turned the lights on I couldn't find him anywhere. After I had hunted for half an hour I noticed a fluttering up on the ceiling above the floor lamp. He had gone to roost on a cross bar of the lamp and it was getting too hot for him after I turned the light on. I turned all the lights off and caught him in my hand.

In the fall when he began to sing, a friend of mine
from Portland said, "Doctor, he is trying to say what
you call him, 'Chicky Boy.'" That first year he learned
to say it very plainly. In a couple of years he would
sing, "Chicky Boy, O Dear Dearie Me, Chicky Baby."
All the words I said to him.

He became very tame and rode about the house on
my shoulder and on the top of my head. Many times
when I lay down on the couch he settled on my forehead or chest for his nap. If I stuck my tongue out at
him he flew across the room and fluttered in my face as
if he were plenty mad.

He dearly loved company. He settled on the back of
a chair and filled the house with "Chicky Boy,"
"Chicky Baby," or "O, Dearie Chicky." I put a lady's
compact in his cage so that he could see himself. He sat
on his pan, a jar lid, and looked at himself in the mirror
by the hour. He often slept in the lid instead of on his
perch.

Dr. Fred Thompson was so charmed that he wanted
me to put another bird in with Chicky Boy to see if he
would teach him to sing. He bought a half-brother canary from my sister and we put them together. They
were both males and seemed happy together. Round and
round through my apartment they flew like two rays of
sunshine. I kept Dr. Thompson's bird fifteen months but
Chicky Boy never said one of his words while the other
bird was there. They thrilled all my friends with their
antics and songs.

After the doctor took his bird home, Chicky Boy flew
through the rooms chirping for his friend who had disappeared. After two years, Dr. Thompson wanted to go
on a vacation and asked me to keep his bird again,

which I did. It was pathetic to see how happy those birds were to be together again. He was here for three weeks until Dr. Thompson took him home. That bird lived only three weeks after that and I have always thought he died from grief.

During World War II Chicky Boy never sang a note. But as soon as the war was over he began to sing again. I do not know why.

At last he was getting on toward twelve years old and I noticed that his song was not as joyous. In the springtime he began to sleep a lot. He took short naps on the curtain pole but gradually slept nearer his cage, then inside his cage.

I always kept a soup bowl in the window full of water so that he could take his bath whenever he chose. He used to take it two or three times a day, but I noticed that he wasn't always able to fly from his bath to his cage without tumbling down onto the floor. I set his cage on a stool near the window where his bath water was so that he didn't have to work so hard. Soon his feathers became gummed up and he just sat in the bottom of his cage. Then one day he managed to take a bath and preen his feathers, but the next morning I found him in the bottom of his cage on his back with his feet up in the air. He lay there like a beautiful yellow flower with its petals folded.

Whenever the paper boy came to collect for the paper he always came indoors to enjoy Chicky Boy. The following day he came and brought another boy to see the bird, but as soon as he came in he asked, "Where is your bird?" When I told him he kept repeating, "I bet you were sorry."

We made records of Chicky Boy's song and whenever children come we put on the record so they can hear the little fellow sing. Some picture heaven paved with gold and marble stairways, but who needs golden pavements or marble stairways?

What we will need is the joyous song of birds. I can never picture heaven without the things that we can love and who could love a pavement?

Epilogue

A Woven Fabric

Life is woven of circumstances and will
circumstances the threads, will the shuttle
weaving ugly rags or fine and beautiful cloth.

Early days of weaving full of knots and smudges,
willfulness, misdirected energy, carelessness.

A cool wind in my face, an inspiration,
   smooth and even.
Color, romance.

Flying fingers push the shuttle.
Joy to love. Joy to be loved.
Unruffled, gently flowing.

I am to be a mother.
A few short months, a tiny morsel in my arms.
I am a mother.

As suddenly,
threads tangle and break.

I cannot see to push the shuttle.
I am a widow.

Not a creature for the world.
I am to carry, to render service.

Not a time for self pity but for weaving.
Broken threads gathered, controlled.

A wide fabric.
Twinkling stars of early morning.
Cobwebs outline a million sparkling dewdrops.
Honey trembles in a primrose challis.
A meadowlark's joyous song.
A hundred prairie chickens feed at daybreak.
Old Prince, my faithful horse, jogs along,
stops in his dusty tracks,
snorts at a firefly in a potato patch.

It was nothing.

The mocking bird sings at midnight.
A vicious stab of lightning,
awesome rolls of thunder.
A dusty wind.
The cold of winter.

Old Prince is supplanted.
Engines take me West:
tall firs in cool and luxuriant fern beds
outline the sky,
blue Cascades in a brilliant morning,
clouds in a misty valley.

Nights of patient vigil.
Behold the miracle of childbirth, again and again
ease the pain of passing from this world.

Golden threads of friendship.
Love in return for their constancy.

—MARY CANAGA ROWLAND

Chronology

RED WILLOW, NE	*June 29, 1873*	Mariam (Mary) Ellen Canaga born to Elias Canaga and Ellen Crockford
KANSAS CITY, MO	*March 26, 1895*	J. Walter Rowland receives M.D. from Kansas City Medical College
HERNDON, KS	*May 23, 1897*	Mary and Walter are married
KANSAS CITY, MO	*March 21, 1901*	Mary receives first M.D. from Woman's Medical College of Kansas City, Missouri
HERNDON, KS	*April 25, 1902*	Nellie born to Mary and Walter
	April 28, 1902	Walter is killed
	1904	Mary marries August Kleint (they separate after a short time and she obtains a divorce in 1909)

OMAHA, NE	*April 19, 1905*	Mary receives second M.D. from John A. Creighton Medicine College
	1905	Travel to Portland, Oregon, and Idaho
TOPEKA, KS	*1905*	Mary practices in Topeka
LONG VALLEY, ID	*1909*	Mary divorces August Kleint and moves to Idaho
LEBANON, OR	*1909*	Mary passes Oregon State Medical Board Examinations
	1910	Mary is licensed to practice medicine in Oregon
	1913	Travel to New York City for study at New York Post-Graduate School
SALEM, OR	*1916*	Mary moves to Salem
	1917	Mary is appointed physician for Chemawa Federal Indian School
	1927	Resigns medical position at Chemawa
	1930–1955	Mary writes memoirs
	August 1, 1966	Mary dies at ninety-three

Glossary

AGUE: a fever with chills, usually malarial.

BILIOUS: pertaining to or consisting of bile; having or resulting from an ailment of the bile or liver; accompanied by headache, indigestion, nausea, etc.

BULBAR PARALYSIS: paralysis of the medulla oblongata, the spinal cord branch into the lowest part of the brain which contains vital nerves controlling bodily functions such as blood circulation and respiration.

CAESAREAN SECTION: delivering a baby surgically through the mother's abdomen; Julius Caesar is said to have been born in this way.

CALOMEL: mercurous chloride, a white tasteless powder formerly used as a cathartic or diuretic; today commonly used in antibacterial ointments.

CAROTID ARTERY: the two large arteries, one on each side of the neck, which carry blood from the aorta to the head.

CHLOROFORM: trichloromethane; colorless volatile liquid of a sweetish taste; organic solvent; used as an anodyne or antispasmodic; formerly used as a surgical anesthetic.

CHOLERA INFANTUM: infectious intestinal disease afflicting infants or young children; occurring in warm

204

weather and caused by severe diarrhea, vomiting, fever, and prostration.

CORONARY THROMBOSIS: coagulation of blood into a clot that obstructs circulation in one of the coronary arteries, leading to a suppression of blood supply to the heart.

CURETTED: to scrape and clean with a curette, a scoop- or spoon-shaped surgical instrument used to remove tissues from the interior of body cavities.

DIPHTHERIA: acute infectious disease of the throat and air passages; symptoms include fever, debilitation, inflammation of the throat, and the formation of a membrane that obstructs breathing.

ENSANGUINATE: to stain or cover with blood; archaic form of ensanguine.

EPSOM SALTS: magnesium sulfate, a white crystalline salt named for the famous mineral waters of Epsom, England; used primarily as a cathartic.

GRAND MAL: in this form of epilepsy the patient is unconscious and undergoes seizures.

ICHTHYOL: oil compound derived from a bituminous mineral containing the remains of fossil fishes.

JIMSON WEED: shortened from Jamestown weed, from Jamestown, Virginia; *Datura stramonium*, poisonous weed of the nightshade family producing stramonium; used in medicine as a narcotic.

MACULES: spots or blotches on the skin, perceptibly at the same level of the surrounding skin.

MALARIAL: related to malaria: an infectious disease, generally recurrent, caused by red blood parasites; transmitted to humans by infected mosquitoes; characterized by severe chills, fever, and anemia.

MEASLES: acute infectious viral disease characterized by skin eruption, fever, and nasal inflammation.

MENINGITIS: inflammation of the meninges—the membranes that envelop the brain and spinal cord—especially as the result of infection by bacteria or viruses; the three forms of meningitis are spinal, cerebral, and cerebrospinal.

OBSTETRICAL: medical instrument resembling a forceps, used to facilitate childbirth.

OCCLUDED: closed, shut, or blocked.

PAPULES: small, usually inflammatory, elevations of the skin.

PERITONSILLAR ABSCESS: an abscess forming in acute tonsillitis around one or more tonsils; quinsy.

PETIT MAL: literally, in French, little sickness; a relatively mild form of epilepsy in which there are short attacks of unconsciousness without convulsions.

PILOCARPINE: an alkaloid extracted from the South American jaborandi plant and used to stimulate sweating.

PLEURAL CAVITY: pertaining to the pleura, a thin serous membrane which covers the inside of the thorax and also envelops the lungs separately, forming two closed sacs.

PNEUMOGASTRIC NERVE: also known as the vagus nerve, either of the tenth pair of cranial nerves, arising in the medulla oblongata and innervating the larynx, lungs, heart, esophagus, and most of the abdominal organs.

QUININE: a bitter crystalline alkaloid extracted from cinchona bark, compounds of which are used especially to treat malaria.

QUINSY: an inflammation of the tonsils, accompanied by the formation of pus.

SCURVY: disease resulting from a deficiency of vitamin
C; symptoms include debilitation, anemia, spongy
gums, bleeding from the mucous membranes.

SMALLPOX: acute infectious viral disease; symptoms include fever, vomiting, and several stages of skin erup-
tions; the resulting pustules eventually dry up and
break, forming soft yellow crusts, then after a week
the scabs fall off leaving pockmarks.

SPECULUM: an instrument used for dilation of a passage
or cavity to facilitate examination.

TUBERCULOSIS: infectious disease caused by the tubercle
bacillus and characterized by the formation of tuber-
cles in various tissues of the body, especially lungs;
other organs may be affected; symptoms include sep-
tic infection, fever, emaciation, and nightsweats.

TYPHOID FEVER: acute infectious disease caused by a
bacillus and acquired through drinking infected liq-
uids; characterized by fever and intestinal disorders.

Index

208

Acknowledgments

The editor would like to thank the following individuals who were instrumental in preparing this manuscript for publication:

Carolyn Madsen Williams of Springfield, Virginia.
Dr. Irving H. Silver, Robert W. Casey, Bill Zimmerman, Michael Carroll, Christopher B. Bumcrot, Michael Kagan, and Rollene Saal of New York City.
Kristin Koskella, Kathirine Loomis, Ken Widmeyer, Dale Hart, Kristin Kennell, John and Liz Dieffenbach, Tom Zachary, Sayre Coombs, Judy Dreis, and Joyce Justice of Seattle, Washington.
Amelia Beth Loomis and Jim Rowlan of Mill Valley, California.
Philip Calder Moore and Jill Holmes of Toronto, Ontario.
Amre Youssef of Jersey City, New Jersey.
Dr. Frank M. Sheridan and Dr. Paula R. Marmont of Shreveport, Louisiana.
Dr. Glenda C. Loomis of Boise, Idaho.
Editha Kleint Emerson of Cascade, Idaho.
Paul R. Kleint of Donnelly, Idaho.

Dr. Bradford W. Gauss and Marcia R. Gauss of McCall, Idaho.
William M. Grace of Topeka, Kansas.
Nancy J. Hulston of Kansas City, Kansas.
Ona F. Malleck and Judy D. Keith of Indianola, Nebraska.

Special thanks to the University of Washington Department of English and Suzzallo Library Map Collection and Cartographic Information Services, Kansas State Historical Society, University of Kansas Medical Center Department of the History and Philosophy of Medicine and Clendening History of Medicine Library, National Archives-Pacific Northwest Region, Seattle Public Library, Idaho State Historical Society, Nebraska State Historical Society, Library of Congress Geography and Map Division, Creighton University, AE Design, Widmeyer Design, and Chief Printing.

    The editor would also like to acknowledge the direction of former teachers: John Griffith and the late Angelo Pellegrini of the University of Washington; Peter S. Hawkins and the late Roland Bainton and Sydney Ahlstrom of Yale University.